Fundamental of Instrumentation and Process Control

Cement Technology

Dr. Rahul Omar

Assistant Professor

Department of Cement Technology

AKS University Satna

NOTION PRESS

NOTION PRESS

India. Singapore. Malaysia.

Preface of the First Edition

I am very glad to present this first edition of the book - Fundamental of instrumentation and process control to students of cement technology.

The subject matter is divided into five chapters and sufficient numbers of illustrative examples are given on each chapter. The entire matter is arranged in proper order with simplified diagram and put in a simple language so that the students of cement technology will understand it very easily.

I am heartily thankful to staff members of cement technology departments located at AKS University Satna (M.P.) for recommending of this book.

I hope positively that students as well as staff members will appreciate the content of the book.

I would welcome and appreciate suggestion and comments from the students and staff members for improving the quality of the book.

Dr. Rahul Omar
Assistant Professor
Department of Cement Technology
AKS University Satna

Dedicated

To

My Parents

Sh. Rakesh Kumar Gupta

&

Smt. Meera Omar

Contents

Chapter 1
General Principles of Process control

1.1. Process control

As competition becomes stiffer in the chemical marketplace and processes become more complicated to operate, it is advantageous to make use of some form of automatic control.

Automatic control of a process offers many advantages, including

- Enhanced process safety
- Satisfying environmental constraints
- Meeting ever-stricter product quality specifications
- More efficient use of raw materials and energy
- Increased profitability

Considering all the benefits that can be realized through process control, it is well worth the time and effort required to become familiar with the concepts and practices used in the field.

1.2. Control systems

Control systems are used to maintain process conditions at their desired values by manipulating certain process variables to adjust the variables of interest. A common example of a control system from everyday life is the cruise control on an automobile.

The purpose of a cruise control is to maintain the speed of the vehicle (the controlled variable) at the desired value (the set point) despite variations in terrain, hills, etc. (disturbances) by adjusting the throttle, or the fuel flow to the engine (the manipulated variable). Another common example is the home hot water heater.

The control system on the hot water heater attempts to maintain the temperature in the tank at the desired value by manipulating the fuel flow to the burner (for a gas heater) or the electrical input to the heater in the face of disturbances such as the varying demand on the heater early in the morning, as it is called upon to provide water for the daily showers.

As the field of process control has matured over the last 30 years, it has become one of the core areas in chemical engineering along with thermodynamics, heat transfer, mass transfer, fluid mechanics, and reactor kinetics.

The literature in process control is enormous: over a dozen textbooks and thousands of papers have been published during the last three decades. This body of knowledge has become so large that it is impossible to cover it all at the undergraduate level. Therefore, we present essential for gaining an understanding of the basic principles of process control.

One of the important themes that we emphasize is the need for control engineers to understand the process-its operation, constraints, design, and objectives. The way the plant is designed has a large impact on how it should be controlled and what level of control performance can be obtained.

We present in the following section three simple examples that illustrate the importance of dynamic response; show the structure of a single-input, single-output conventional control system; and illustrate a typical plant wide control system.

Throughout, many more real-life examples and problems are presented. All of these are drawn from close to 50 years of collective experience of the authors in solving practical control problems in the chemical and petroleum industries.

1.3. Examples of process dynamics and control

EXAMPLE 1: **Figure1.1** shows a tank into which an incompressible (constant-density) liquid is pumped at a variable rate F_o (gal/min). This inflow rate can vary with time because of changes in operations upstream. The height of liquid in the vertical cylindrical tank is h (ft). The flow rate out of the tank is F (gal/min). Now F_o, h, and F will all vary with time and are therefore functions of time 1.

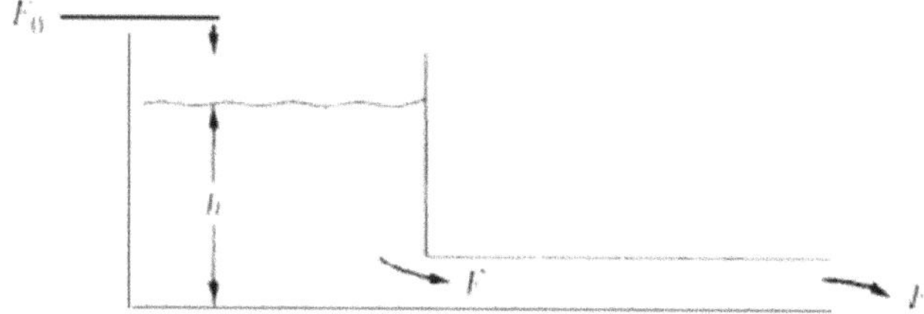

Figure1.1: Liquid tank

Consequently, we use the notation $Fo_{(t)}$, $h_{(t)}$, and $F_{(t)}$. Liquid leaves the base of the tank via a long horizontal pipe and discharges into the top of another tank. Both tanks are open to the atmosphere.

Let us look first at the steady-state conditions. By "steady state" we mean the conditions when nothing is changing with time or when time has become very large. Mathematically this corresponds to having all time derivatives equal to zero or allowing time to approach infinity.

At steady state the flow rate out of the tank must equal the flow rate into the tank: $F_o = F$. In this book we denote the steady-state value of a variable by an over score or bar.

For a given F, the height of liquid in the tank at steady state h is a constant, and a larger flow rate requires a higher liquid level.

The liquid height provides just enough hydraulic pressure head at the inlet of the pipe to overcome the frictional pressure losses of the liquid flowing down the pipe.

The steady-state design of the tank involves the selection of the height and diameter of the tank and the diameter of the exit pipe. For a given pipe diameter, the tank height must be large enough to prevent the tank from overflowing at the maximum expected flow rate.

Thus, the design involves an engineering trade-off, i.e., an economic balance between the cost of a taller tank and the cost of a bigger-diameter pipe. A larger pipe diameter requires a lower liquid height. A conservative design engineer would probably include a 20 to 30 percent over-design factor in the tank height to permit future capacity increases. Safety and environmental reviews would probably recommend the installation of a high-level alarm and/or an interlock (a device to shut off the feed if the level gets too high) to guarantee that the tank could never overfill.

The tragic accidents at Three Mile Island, Chernobyl, and Bhopal illustrate the need for well-designed and well-instrumented Plants.

EXAMPLE 2: Consider the heat exchanger sketched in **Figure1.2**. An oil stream passes through the tube side of a tube-in-shell heat exchanger and is heated by condensing steam on the shell side. The steam condensate leaves through a steam trap (a device that permits only liquid to pass through it, thus preventing "blow-through" of the steam vapor).

We want to control the temperature of the oil leaving the heat exchanger. To do this, a thermocouple is inserted in a thermo well in the exit oil pipe. The thermocouple wires are connected to a "temperature transmitter," an electronic device that converts the millivolt thermocouple output to a 4- to 20-mA "control signal."

This current signal is sent to a temperature controller, an electronic, digital, or pneumatic device that compares the desired temperature (the "set point") with the actual temperature and sends out a signal to a control valve. The temperature controller opens the steam valve a little if the temperature is too low and closes the valve a little if the temperature is too high.

We consider all the components of this temperature control loop in more detail. For now we need only appreciate the fact that the automatic control of some variable in a process requires the installation of a sensor, a transmitter, a controller, and a final control element (usually a control valve).

A major component involves learning how to decide what type of controller should be used and how it should be "tuned," i.e., how the adjustable tuning parameters in the controller should be set so that we do a good control job.

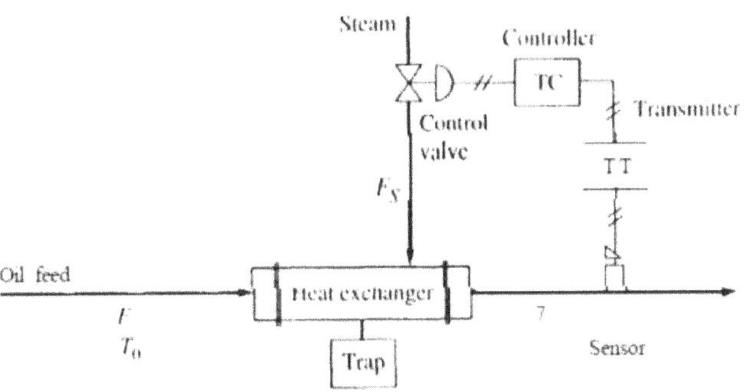

Figure1.2: Heat exchanger sketched

1.4. Feedback Control

The control system shown in Figure1.3 is called a *closed-loop* system or a feedback system because the measured value of the controlled variable is returned or "feedback" to a device called the *comparator.* In the comparator, the controlled variable is compared with the desired value or *set point.* If there is any difference between the measured variable and the set point, an error is generated. This error enters a *controller,* which in turn adjusts the *final control element* to return the controlled variable to the set point.

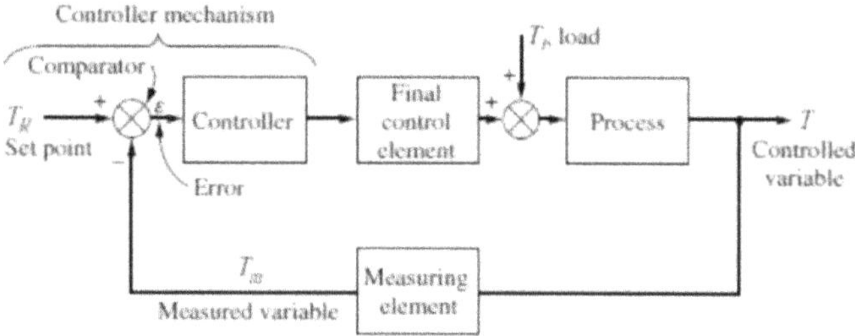

Figure1.3: Block diagram of a simple control system

As discussed above, the controller is to do the same job that the human operator was to do, except that the controller is told in advance exactly how to do it. This means that the controller will use the existing values of T and T_R to adjust the heat input according to a predetermined formula.

Let the difference between these temperatures, $T_R - T,$ be called error. Clearly, the larger this error, the less we are satisfied with the present state of affairs and vice versa.

In fact, we are completely satisfied only when the error is exactly zero.

Based on these considerations, it is natural to suggest that the controller should change the heat input by an amount **proportional** to the error. Thus, a plausible formula for the controller to follow is

$$q(t) = wC(T_R - T_{is}) + K_c(T_R - T) \qquad (1.1)$$

where K_c is a (positive) constant of proportionality. This is called **proportional control.** In effect, the controller is instructed to maintain the heat input at the steady-state design value q_s as long as T is equal to T_R, i.e., as long as the error is zero. If T deviates from T_R, causing an error, the controller is to use the magnitude of the error to change the heat input proportionally.

We shall reserve the right to vary the parameter K, to suit our needs. This degree of freedom forms a part of our instructions to the controller.

The concept of using information about the deviation of the system from its desired state to control the system is called feedback control. Information about the state of the system is "fed back" to a controller, which utilizes this information to change the system in some way. In the present case, the information is the temperature T and the change is made in

q. When the term $\mathbf{wC(T_R - }\mathit{T_{is}})$ is abbreviated to q_s, becomes

$$q = q_s + K_c(T_R - T) \qquad (1.2)$$

1.5. Feed forward control

If a particular load disturbance occurs frequently in a control process, the quality of control can often be improved by the addition of feed forward control. Consider the composition control system in which a concentrated stream of control reagent containing water and solute is used to control the concentration of the stream leaving a three-tank system.

The stream to be processed passes through a preconditioning stirred tank where composition fluctuations are smoothed out before the outlet stream is mixed with control reagent. A three-tank system has been chosen for ease of computation in a numerical example that follows.

If the change in load disturbance C_i can be detected as soon as it occurs in the inlet stream, this information can be fed forward to a second controller that adjusts the control valve in such a way as to prevent any change in the outlet composition from the set point.

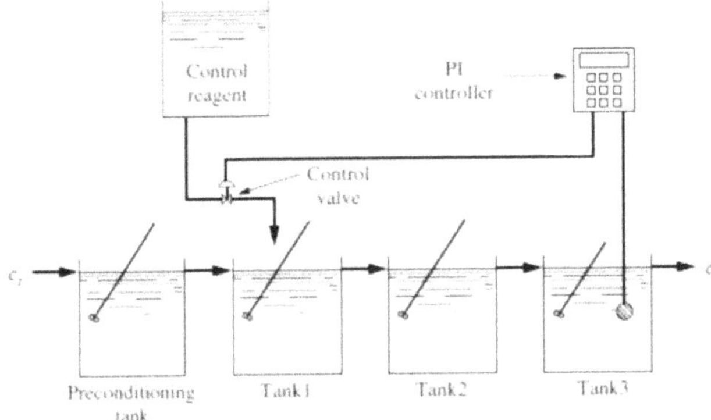

Figure1.4: Composition control system: physical process

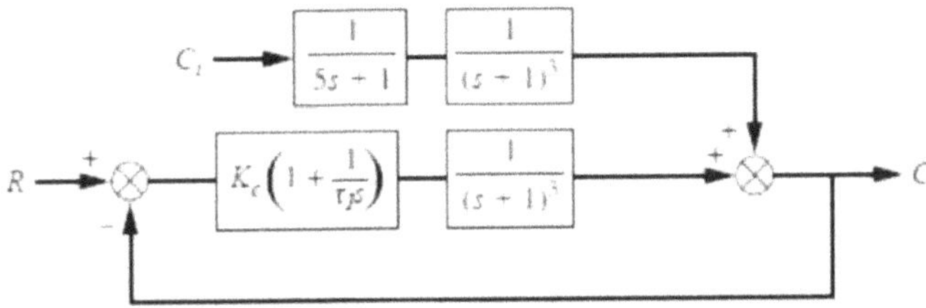

Figure1.5: Composition control system: block diagram

A controller that uses information fed forward from the source of the load disturbance is called a *feed forward* controller. The block diagram that includes the feed forward controller G_f as well as the feedback controller G_c.

1.6. Analysis of Feed forward Control

The response of C to changes in C_i and R can be written as follows:

$$C(s) = G_1(s)G_p(s)C_i(s) + G_f(s)G_p(s)C_i(s) + G_c(s)G_p(s)E(s)$$

$$(1.3)$$

Where $E(s) = R(s) - C(s)$.

To determine the transfer function of $G f(s)$ that will prevent any change in the control variable C from its set point R, which is 0, we solve for $G_f(s)$ with $C = 0$ and $R = 0$. The result is

$$G_f(s) = -G_1(s)$$

(1.4)

1.7. Implementing Feed forward Transfer Functions

In applications of feed forward control, $G_f(s)$ may take the form of a lead expression, such as $G_f(s) = 1 + t_f s$. When this occurs, it is necessary to approximate $1 + t_f s$ by a lead-lag expression, such as

$$G_f(s) = \frac{1 + \tau_f s}{1 + \beta \tau_f s}$$

(1.5)

1.8. Response of First order system

It is necessary to become familiar with the responses of some of the simple, basic systems that often are the building blocks of a control system. This chapter and the three that follow describe in detail the behavior of several basic systems and show that a great variety of physical systems can be represented by a combination of these basic systems. Some of the terms and conventions that have become well established in the field of automatic control will also be introduced.

1.9. Transfer function of First order system

Mercury thermometer: We develop the *transfer function* for a *first-order system* by considering the unsteady-state behavior of an ordinary mercury-in-glass thermometer. A cross-sectional view of the bulb is shown in Figure 1.6.

Consider the thermometer to be located in a flowing stream of fluid for which the temperature x varies with time. Our problem is to calculate the *response* or the time variation of the thermometer reading y for a particular change in x. *(In order that the result of the analysis of the thermometer be general and therefore applicable to other first-order systems, the symbols x and y have been selected to represent surrounding temperature and thermometer reading, respectively.)*

The following assumptions will be used in this analysis:

1. All the resistance to heat transfer resides in the film surrounding the bulb (i.e., the resistance offered by the glass and mercury is neglected).

2. All the thermal capacity is in the mercury. Furthermore, at any instant the mercury assumes a uniform temperature throughout.

3. The glass wall containing the mercury does not expand or contract during the transient response. (In an actual thermometer, the expansion of the wall has an additional effect on the response of the thermometer reading. The glass initially expands and the cavity containing the mercury grows, resulting in mercury reading that initially falls. Once the mercury warms and expands the reading increases. This is an example of an inverse response.

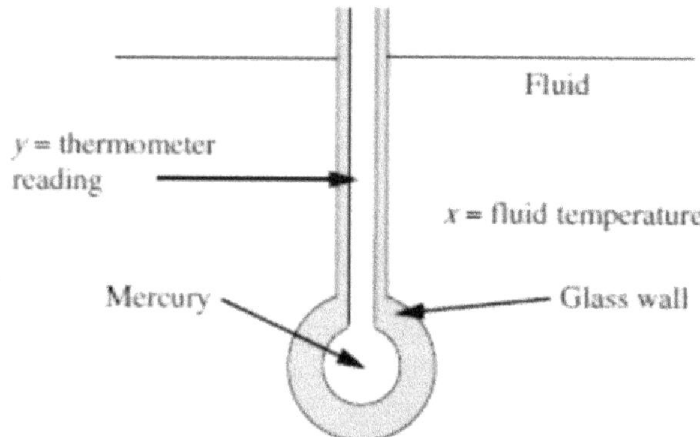

Figure1.6: Cross-sectional view of thermometer

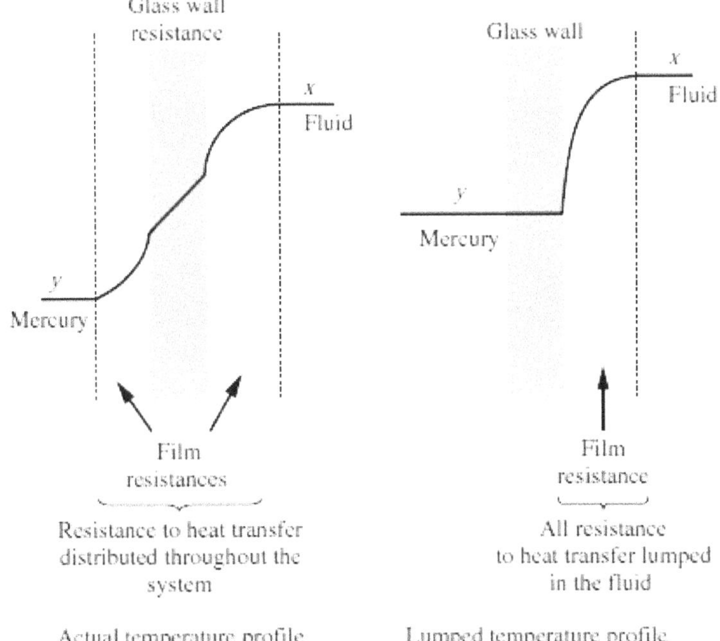

Figure1.7: Temperature profiles in thermometer

It is assumed that the thermometer is initially at steady state. This means that, before time 0, there is no change in temperature with time. At time 0, the thermometer will be subjected to some change in the surrounding temperature x (t).

By applying the unsteady-state energy balance

(Input rate) – (Output rate) = (Rate of accumulation)

We get the result

$$hA(x - y) - 0 = mC\frac{dy}{dt}$$

(1.6)

Where

A = surface area of bulb for heat transfer, ft^2

C = heat capacity of mercury, Btu/ ($lb_m \cdot °F$)

m = mass of mercury in bulb, lb_m

t = time, h

h = film coefficient of heat transfer, Btu/ ($ft^2 \cdot h \cdot °F$)

1.10. Physical examples of First order system

1.10.1. Liquid Level

Consider the system shown in Figure 1.8, which consists of a tank of uniform cross-sectional area A to which is attached a flow resistance R such as a valve, a pipe, or a weir. Assume that q_o, the volumetric flow rate (volume/time) through the resistance, is related to the head h by the linear relationship:

$$q_o = \frac{h}{R}$$

$$(1.7)$$

A resistance that has this linear relationship between flow and head is referred to as a *linear resistance.* (A pipe is a linear resistance if the flow is in the laminar range. A specially contoured weir, called a Sutro weir, produces a linear head-flow relationship. Turbulent flow through pipes and valves is generally proportional to $\sqrt{h}$.

Flow through weirs having simple geometric shapes can be expressed as Kh^n, where K and n are positive constants. For example, the flow through a rectangular weir is proportional to $h^{3/2}$).

A time-varying volumetric flow q of liquid of constant density r enters the tank. Determine the transfer function that relates head to flow. We can analyse this system by writing a transient mass balance around the tank:

$$\begin{pmatrix} \text{Rate of} \\ \text{mass flow in} \end{pmatrix} - \begin{pmatrix} \text{Rate of} \\ \text{mass flow out} \end{pmatrix} = \begin{pmatrix} \text{Rate of accumulation} \\ \text{of mass in tank} \end{pmatrix} \tag{1.8}$$

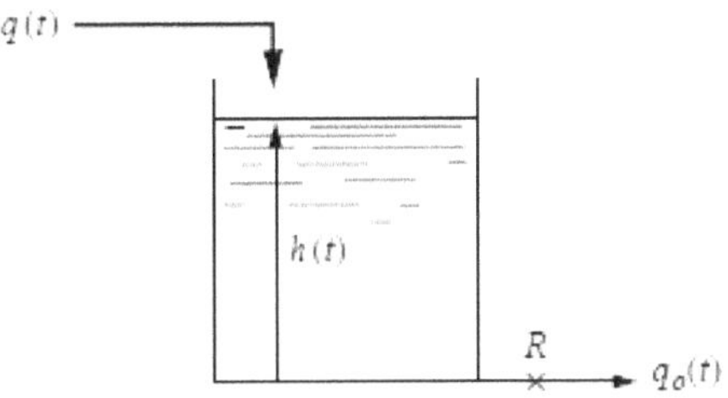

Figure1.8: Liquid-Level tank

Notice that the steady-state gain for this transfer function is dimensionless, which is to be expected because the input variable $q\,(t)$ and the output variable $q_o\,(t)$ have the same units (volume/time). The possibility of approximating an impulse forcing function in the flow rate to the liquid-level system is quite real.

Recall that the unit-impulse function is defined as a pulse of unit area as the duration of the pulse approaches zero, and the impulse function can be approximated by suddenly increasing the flow to a large value for a very short time; that is, we may pour very quickly a volume of liquid into the tank. The nature of the impulse response for a liquid-level system will be described by the following example.

$$\frac{Q_o(s)}{Q(s)} = \frac{1}{\tau s + 1}$$

(1.9)

1.10.2. Liquid-Level Process with Constant-Flow Outlet

An example of a transfer function that often arises in control systems may be developed by considering the liquid-level system shown in Figure 1.9.

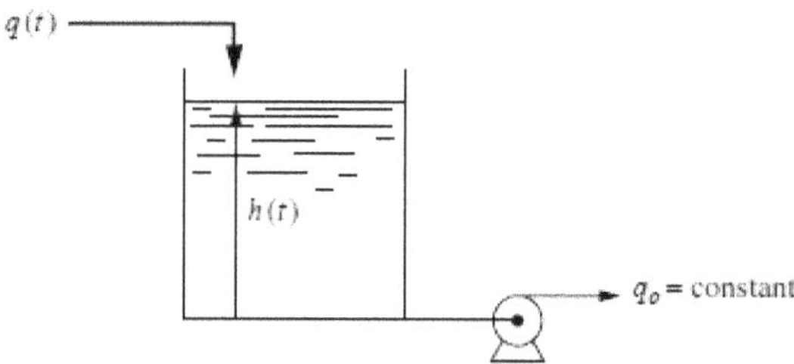

Figure1.9: Liquid-Level Process

The transfers function for the liquid-level system with constant outlet flow given by as $R \to \infty$.

$$\lim_{R \to \infty} \left(\frac{R}{ARs + 1} \right) = \frac{1}{As}$$

(1.10)

1.10.3. Mixing Process

Consider the mixing process shown in Figure 1.10 in which a stream of solution containing dissolved salt flows at a constant volumetric flow rate q into a tank of constant holdup volume V. The concentration of the salt in the entering stream x (mass of salt/volume) varies with time.

It is desired to determine the transfer function relating the outlet concentration y to the inlet concentration x. If we assume the density of the solution to be constant, the flow rate in must equal the flow rate out, since the holdup volume is fixed.

We may analyses this system by writing a transient mass balance for the salt; thus

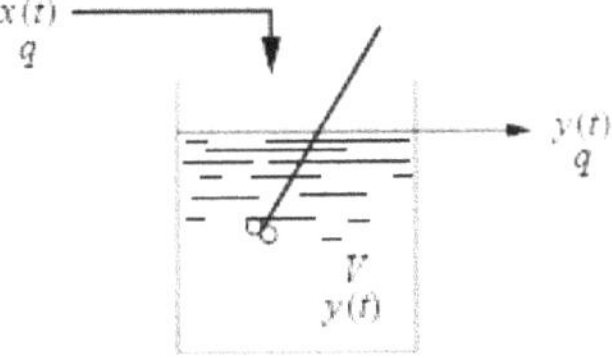

Figure1.10: Mixing Process

$$\begin{pmatrix} \text{Flow rate of} \\ \text{salt in} \end{pmatrix} - \begin{pmatrix} \text{Flow rate of} \\ \text{salt out} \end{pmatrix} = \begin{pmatrix} \text{Rate of accumulation} \\ \text{of salt in tank} \end{pmatrix}$$

(1.11)

$$\frac{Y(s)}{X(s)} = \frac{1}{\tau s + 1}$$

(1.12)

Where $\tau = V / q$.

This mixing process is, therefore, another first-order process for which the dynamics are now well known.

1.10.4. Heating Process

Consider the heating process shown in Figure 1.11. A stream at temperature T_i is fed to the tank. Heat is added to the tank by means of an electric heater. The tank is well mixed, and the temperature of the exiting stream is T. The flow rate to the tank is constant at w lb/h. A transient energy balance on the tank Yields.

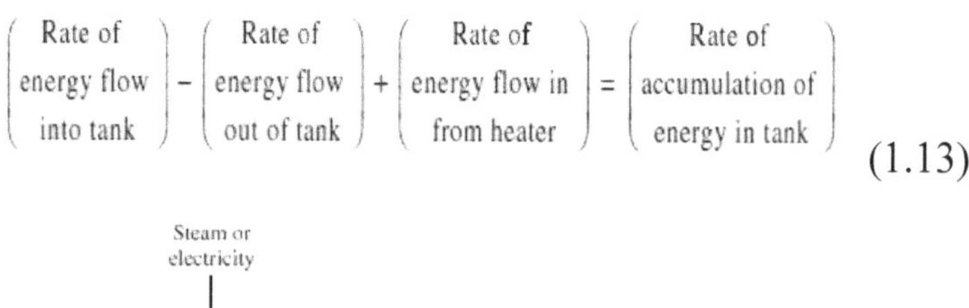

$$\begin{pmatrix} \text{Rate of} \\ \text{energy flow} \\ \text{into tank} \end{pmatrix} - \begin{pmatrix} \text{Rate of} \\ \text{energy flow} \\ \text{out of tank} \end{pmatrix} + \begin{pmatrix} \text{Rate of} \\ \text{energy flow in} \\ \text{from heater} \end{pmatrix} = \begin{pmatrix} \text{Rate of} \\ \text{accumulation of} \\ \text{energy in tank} \end{pmatrix}$$

(1.13)

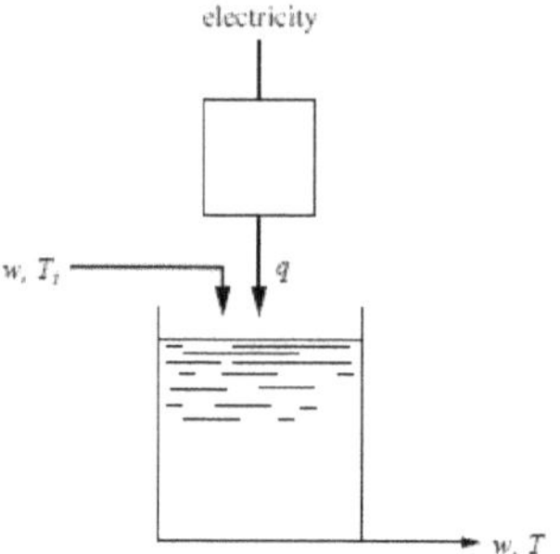

Figure 1.11: Heating Process

Thus, this process exhibits first-order dynamics as the tank temperature T responds to changes in the heat input to the tank.

$$\frac{T'(s)}{Q(s)} = \frac{1/wC}{(\rho V/w)s + 1} = \frac{K}{\tau s + 1}$$

(1.14)

1.11. Response of First order system in series - Non-interacting system

As in the previous liquid-level example, we shall assume the liquid to be of constant density, the tanks to have uniform cross-sectional area, and the flow resistances to be linear. Our problem is to find a transfer function that relates $h2$ to q, that is, $H2$ $(s)/Q(s)$.

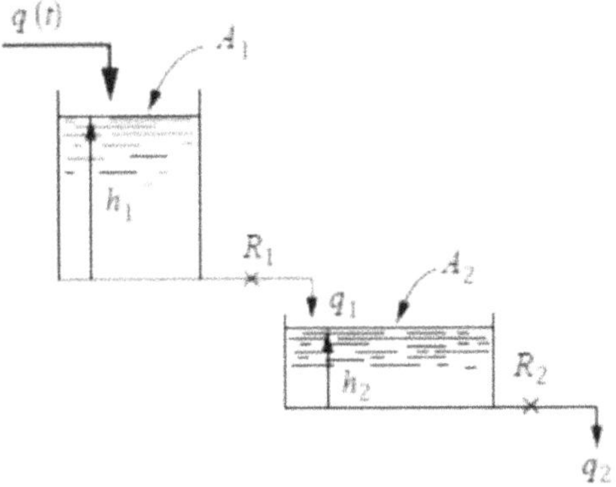

Figure 1.12: Two-tank liquid-level system: Non-interacting

The approach will be to obtain a transfer function for each tank, $Q1(s)/Q(s)$ and $H2\,(s)/Q1(s)$, by writing a transient mass balance around each tank; these transfer functions will then be combined to eliminate the intermediate flow $Q1(s)$ and produce the desired transfer function. A balance on tank 1 gives

$$q - q_1 = A_1 \frac{dh_1}{dt}$$

(1.15)

Notice that the overall transfer function of Equation is the product of two first-order transfer functions, each of which is the transfer function of a single tank operating independently of the other.

$$\frac{H_2(s)}{Q(s)} = \frac{1}{\tau_1 s + 1} \frac{R_2}{\tau_2 s + 1}$$

(1.16)

1.12. Generalization for Several Non-interacting Systems in Series

We have observed that the overall transfer function for two non-interacting first-order systems connected in series is simply the product of the individual transfer functions. We may now generalize this concept by considering n non-interacting first-order systems as represented by the block diagram of Figure 1.13.

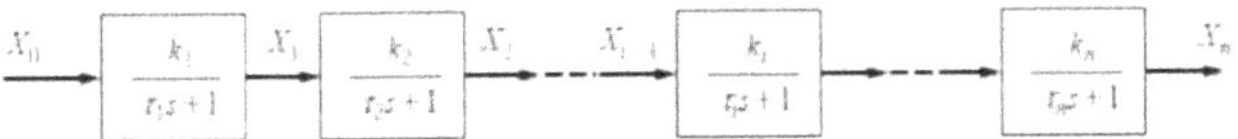

Figure1.13: Non-interacting first-order systems

The block diagram is equivalent to the relationships

$$\frac{X_1(s)}{X_0(s)} = \frac{k_1}{\tau_1 s + 1} \tag{1.17}$$

$$\frac{X_2(s)}{X_1(s)} = \frac{k_2}{\tau_2 s + 1} \tag{1.18}$$

$$\frac{X_n(s)}{X_{n-1}(s)} = \frac{k_n}{\tau_n s + 1} \tag{1.19}$$

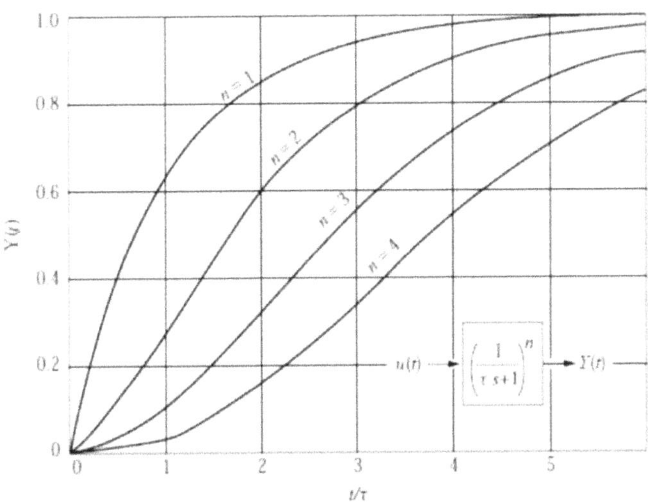

Figure1.14: Step response of non-interacting first-order systems in series

To obtain the overall transfer function, we simply multiply the individual transfer functions;

23

Thus

$$\frac{X_n(s)}{X_0(s)} = \prod_{i=1}^{n} \frac{k_i}{\tau_i s + 1}$$

$$(1.20)$$

To show how the transfer lag is increased as the number of stages increases, Figure1.14 gives the unit-step response curves for several systems containing one or more first order stages in series.

1.13. Response of First order system in series - interacting system

To illustrate an interacting system, we will derive the transfer function for the system shown in Figure 1.15. The analysis is started by writing mass balances on the tanks as was done for the non-interacting case. The balances on tanks 1 and 2 are the same as before and are given by Equations.

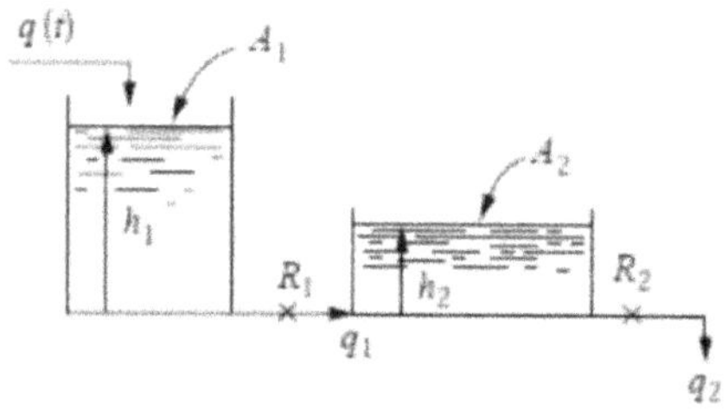

Figure1.15: Two-tank liquid-level system: interacting Tank1

$$q - q_1 = A_1 \frac{dh_1}{dt}$$

$$(1.21)$$

Tank 2

$$q_1 - q_2 = A_2 \frac{dh_2}{dt}$$

$$(1.22)$$

However, the flow-head relationship for R_1 is now

$$q_1 = \frac{1}{R_1}(h_1 - h_2)$$

$$(1.23)$$

The flow-head relationship for $R\,2$ is the same as before

$$q_2 = \frac{h_2}{R_2}$$

$$(1.24)$$

A simple way to combine Equations (1.21), (1.22), (1.23), and (1.24) is to first express them in terms of deviation variables, transform the resulting equations, and then combine the transformed equations to eliminate the unwanted variables.

At steady state, Eqs. (1.21) and (1.22) can be written

$$q_s - q_{1s} = 0$$

$$(1.25)$$

$$q_{1s} - q_{2s} = 0$$

$$(1.26)$$

Subtracting Eq. (1.25) from Eq. (1.21) and Eq. (1.26) from Eq. (1.22) and introducing deviation variables give

Tank 1
$$Q - Q_1 = A_1 \frac{dH_1}{dt}$$
(1.27)

Tank 2
$$Q_1 - Q_2 = A_2 \frac{dH_2}{dt}$$
(1.28)

Expressing Equations (1.23) and (1.24) in terms of deviation variables gives

Valve 1
$$Q_1 = \frac{H_1 - H_2}{R_1}$$
(1.29)

Valve 2
$$Q_2 = \frac{H_2}{R_2}$$
(1.30)

Transforming Equations (1.27) through (1.30) gives

Tank 1
$$Q(s) - Q_1(s) = A_1 s H_1(s)$$
(1.31)

Tank 2
$$Q_1(s) - Q_2(s) = A_2 s H_2(s)$$
(1.32)

Tank 2
$$Q_1(s) - Q_2(s) = A_2 s H_2(s)$$
(1.33)

Valve 2
$$R_2 Q_2(s) = H_2(s)$$
(1.34)

The analysis has produced four algebraic equations containing five unknowns: Q, Q_1, Q_2, H_1, and H_2. These equations may be combined to eliminate Q_1, Q_2, and H_1 and to arrive at the desired transfer function:

$$\frac{H_2(s)}{Q(s)} = \frac{R_2}{\tau_1 \tau_2 s^2 + (\tau_1 + \tau_2 + A_1 R_2)s + 1}$$

$$(1.35)$$

To understand the effect of interaction on the transient response of a system, consider a two-tank system for which the time constants are equal ($\tau_1 = \tau_2 = \tau$). If the tanks are non-interacting, the transfer function relating inlet flow to outlet flow is

$$\frac{Q_2(s)}{Q(s)} = \left(\frac{1}{\tau s + 1}\right)^2$$

$$(1.36)$$

The unit-step response for this transfer function can be obtained by the usual procedure to give

$$Q_2(t) = 1 - e^{-t/\tau} - \frac{t}{\tau}e^{-t/\tau}$$

$$(1.37)$$

If the tanks are interacting, the overall transfer function, according to Eq. (1.35), is (Assuming further that $A_1 = A_2$)

$$\frac{Q_2(s)}{Q(s)} = \frac{1}{\tau^2 s^2 + 3\tau s + 1}$$

$$(1.38)$$

By application of the quadratic formula, the denominator of this transfer function can be written as

$$\frac{Q_2(s)}{Q(s)} = \frac{1}{(0.38\tau s + 1)(2.62\tau s + 1)}$$

$$(1.39)$$

1.14. Second order system - transfer functions

This section introduces a basic system called a *second-order system* or a *quadratic lag*. Second-order systems are described by a second-order differential equation that relates the output variable y to the input variable x (the forcing function) with time as the independent variable.

$$A\frac{d^2 y}{dt^2} + B\frac{dy}{dt} + Cy = x(t)$$

(1.40)

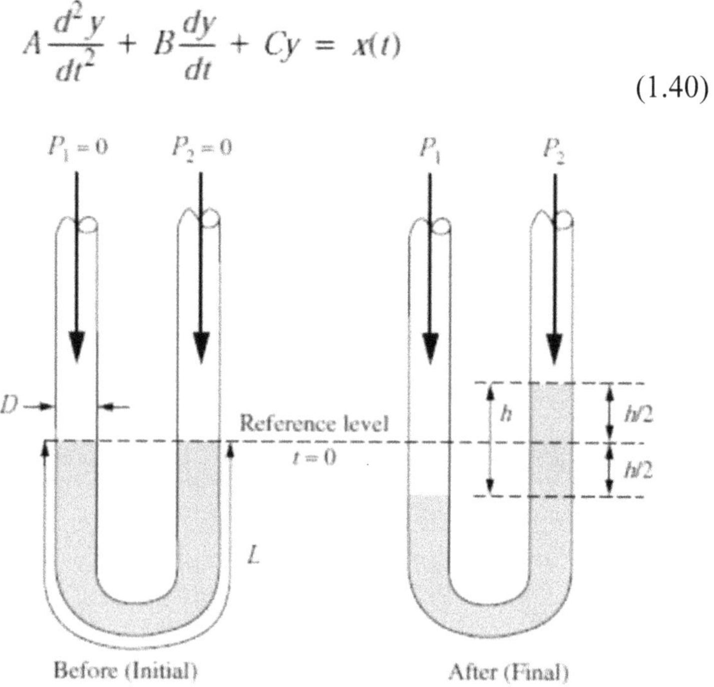

Figure1.16: Manometer for Second order system

A second-order system can arise from two first-order systems in series. Some systems are inherently second-order, and they do not result from a series combination of two first order systems. Inherently second-

28

order systems are not extremely common in chemical engineering applications. Most second-order systems that we encounter will result from the addition of a controller to a first-order process.

Let's examine an inherently second-order system and develop some terminology that will be useful in our analysis of the control of chemical processes. Consider a simple manometer as shown in Figure 1.16.

The pressure on both legs of the manometer is initially the same. The length of the fluid column in the manometer is L. At time $t = 0$, a pressure difference is imposed across the legs of the manometer.

Assuming the resulting flow in the manometer to be laminar and the steady-state friction law for drag force in laminar flow to apply at each instant, we will determine the transfer function between the applied pressure difference ΔP and the manometer reading h.

If we perform a momentum balance on the fluid in the manometer, we arrive at the following terms:
(Sum of forces causing fluid to move) = (R ate of change of momentum of fluid)
Where,

$$\begin{pmatrix} \text{Sum of forces} \\ \text{causing fluid to move} \end{pmatrix} = \begin{pmatrix} \text{Unbalanced pressure forces} \\ \text{causing motion} \end{pmatrix} - \begin{pmatrix} \text{Frictional forces} \\ \text{opposing motion} \end{pmatrix} \tag{1.41}$$

$$\begin{pmatrix} \text{Unbalanced pressure forces} \\ \text{causing motion} \end{pmatrix} = (P_1 - P_2)\frac{\pi D^2}{4} - \rho g h\frac{\pi D^2}{4}$$

(1.42)

$$\begin{pmatrix} \text{Frictional forces} \\ \text{opposing motion} \end{pmatrix} = \begin{pmatrix} \text{Skin friction} \\ \text{at wall} \end{pmatrix} = \begin{pmatrix} \text{Shear stress} \\ \text{at wall} \end{pmatrix} \times \begin{pmatrix} \text{Area in contact} \\ \text{with wall} \end{pmatrix}$$

(1.43)

$$\begin{pmatrix} \text{Frictional forces} \\ \text{opposing motion} \end{pmatrix} = \tau_{\text{Wall}}(\pi D L) = \frac{8\mu \overline{V}}{D}(\pi D L) = \left(\frac{8\mu}{D}\right)\left(\frac{1}{2}\frac{dh}{dt}\right)(\pi D L)$$

(1.44)

The transfer function follows:

$$\frac{Y(s)}{X(s)} = \frac{1}{\tau^2 s^2 + 2\zeta\tau s + 1}$$

(1.45)

Where,

$$\tau = \sqrt{\frac{2L}{3g}} \; \text{s}$$

(1.46)

$$\zeta = \frac{8\mu}{\rho D^2}\sqrt{\frac{3L}{2g}} \; \text{dimensionless}$$

(1.47)

The transfer function given by Equation is written in standard form, and we will show later that other physical systems can be represented by a transfer function having the denominator of

$$\tau^2 s^2 + 2\zeta\tau s + 1$$

(1.48)

All such systems are defined as second-order. Note that it requires two parameters, τ and ζ, to characterize the dynamics of a second-order system in contrast to only one parameter for a first-order system. We now discuss the response of a second-order system to some of the common forcing functions, namely, step, impulse, and sinusoidal.

1.15. Examples of second order systems

Step Response: If the forcing function is a unit-step function, we have

$$X(s) = \frac{1}{s} \tag{1.49}$$

Superposition will enable us to determine easily the response to a step function of any other magnitude. Combining above equation with the transfer function gives

$$Y(s) = \frac{1}{s}\frac{1}{\tau^2 s^2 + 2\zeta\tau s + 1} \tag{1.50}$$

The quadratic term in this equation may be factored into two linear terms that contain the roots

$$s_a = -\frac{\zeta}{\tau} + \frac{\sqrt{\zeta^2 - 1}}{\tau} \tag{1.51}$$

$$s_b = -\frac{\zeta}{\tau} + \frac{\sqrt{\zeta^2 - 1}}{\tau} \tag{1.52}$$

Equation (1.50) can now be written

$$Y(s) = \frac{1/\tau^2}{s(s - s_a)(s - s_b)} \tag{1.53}$$

The response of the system $Y(t)$ can be found by inverting Eq. (1.53). The roots s_a and s_b will be real or complex depending on value of the parameter ζ. The nature of the roots will, in turn, affect the form of $Y(t)$. The problem may be divided into the three cases shown in Table 1.1. Each case will now be discussed.

Table 1.1: Step response of a second-order system

Case	ζ	Nature of roots	Description of response
I	< 1	Complex	Underdamped or oscillatory
II	$= 1$	Real and equal	Critically damped
III	> 1	Real	Overdamped or nonoscillatory

CASE I

Step response for $\zeta < 1$.

For this case, the inversion of Eq. (1.53) yields the result

$$Y(t) = 1 - \frac{1}{\sqrt{1-\zeta^2}} e^{-\zeta t/\tau} \sin\left(\sqrt{1-\zeta^2}\, \frac{t}{\tau} + \tan^{-1} \frac{\sqrt{1-\zeta^2}}{\zeta} \right) \tag{1.54}$$

The constants C_1, C_2, and C_3 are found by partial fractions. The resulting equation is then put in the form of Eq. (1.54) by applying the trigonometric identity. It is evident from Eq. (1.54) that $Y(t) \to 1$ as $t \to \infty$.

The nature of the response can be understood most clearly by plotting the solution to Eq. (1.53), where $Y(t)$ is plotted against the dimensionless variable t/τ for several values of ζ, including those above unity.

Note that for $\zeta < 1$ all the response curves are oscillatory in nature and become less oscillatory as ζ is increased. The slope at the origin is zero for all values of ζ. The response of a second-order system for $\zeta < 1$ is said to be *under damped*.

What is the physical significance of an under damped response? Using the manometer as an example, if we step-change the pressure difference across an under damped manometer, the liquid levels in the two legs will oscillate.

CASE II

STEP RESPONSE FOR $\zeta = 1$.

For this case, the response is given by the Expression

$$Y(t) = 1 - \left(1 + \frac{t}{\tau}\right)e^{-t/\tau}$$

$$(1.55)$$

This is derived as follows: Equations (1.51) and (1.52) show that the roots s_1 and s_2 are real and equal. It is seen that Eq. (1.55) is the correct form. The constants are obtained, as usual, by partial fractions.

The response is non-oscillatory. This condition, $\zeta = 1$, is called *critical damping* and allows the most rapid approach of the response to $Y = 1$ without oscillation.

CASE III

Step response for $\zeta > 1$.

For this case, the inversion of Eq. (5) gives the result

$$Y(t) = 1 - e^{-\zeta t/\tau}\left(\cosh\sqrt{\zeta^2-1}\,\frac{t}{\tau} + \frac{\zeta}{\sqrt{\zeta^2-1}}\sinh\sqrt{\zeta^2-1}\,\frac{t}{\tau}\right) \tag{1.56}$$

Where the hyperbolic functions are defined as:

$$\sinh a = \frac{e^a - e^{-a}}{2} \tag{1.57}$$

$$\cosh a = \frac{e^a + e^{-a}}{2} \tag{1.58}$$

The procedure for obtaining Eq. (1.56) is parallel to that used in the previous cases. The response has been several values of ζ. Notice that the response is non-oscillatory and becomes more "sluggish" as ζ increases.

This is known as an *over damped* response. As in previous cases, all curves eventually approach the line $Y = 1$.

Actually, the response for $\zeta > 1$ is not new. We saw it previously in the discussion of the step response of a system containing two first-order systems in series, for which the transfer function is

$$\frac{Y(s)}{X(s)} = \frac{1}{(\tau_1 s + 1)(\tau_2 s + 1)} \tag{1.59}$$

This is true for $\zeta > 1$ because the roots s_1 and s_2 are real, and the denominator of transfer function may be factored into two real linear factors. Therefore, transfer function is equivalent to Eq. (1.59) in this case. By comparing the linear factors of the denominator of transfer function with those of Eq. (1.59), it follows that

$$\tau_1 = \left(\zeta + \sqrt{\zeta^2 - 1} \right)\tau$$

$$(1.60)$$

$$\tau_2 = \left(\zeta - \sqrt{\zeta^2 - 1} \right)\tau$$

$$(1.61)$$

Note that if $\tau_1 = \tau_2$, then $\tau = \tau_1 = \tau_2$ and $\zeta = 1$.

Chapter 2
Mode of control system

2.1. Mode of control systems

Control systems are used to maintain process conditions at their desired values by manipulating certain process variables to adjust the variables of interest. A common example of a control system from everyday life is the cruise control on an automobile.

The purpose of a cruise control is to maintain the speed of the vehicle (the controlled variable) at the desired value (the set point) despite variations in terrain, hills, etc. (disturbances) by adjusting the throttle, or the fuel flow to the engine (the manipulated variable). Another common example is the home hot water heater.

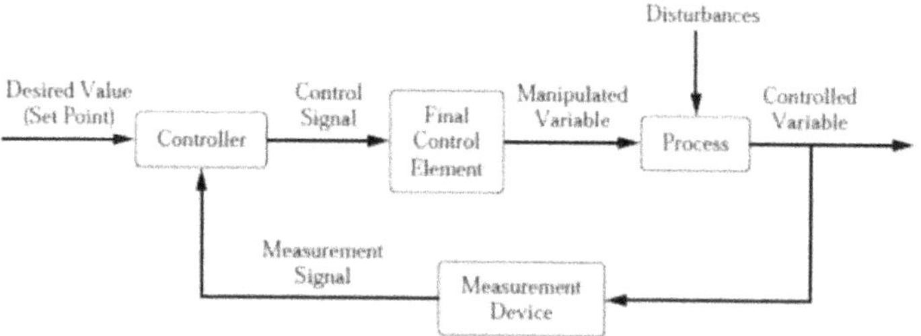

Figure2.1: Generalized process control system

The control system on the hot water heater attempts to maintain the temperature in the tank at the desired value by manipulating the fuel flow to the burner (for a gas heater) or the electrical input to the heater in the face of disturbances such as the varying demand on the heater early in the morning, as it is called upon to provide water for the daily showers.

A third example is the home thermostat. This control system is designed to maintain the temperature in the home at a comfortable value by manipulating the fuel flow or electrical input to the furnace.

The furnace control system must deal with a variety of disturbances to maintain temperature in the house, such as heat losses, doors being opened and hopefully closed, and leaky inefficient windows. The furnace must also be able to respond to a request to raise the desired temperature if necessary. For example, we might desire to raise the temperature by 5°, and we'd like the system to respond smoothly and efficiently.

• The ability to maintain the process variable at its desired value in spite of disturbances that might be experienced (this is termed *disturbance rejection*)

• The ability to move the process variable from one setting to a new desired setting (this is termed *set point tracking*)

The controller compares the measurement signal of the controlled variable to the set point (the desired value of the controlled variable). The difference between the two values is called the *error.*

Error Set = (point value) - (Measurement signal of controlled variable)

The system may be divided into the following components:

1. Process (stirred-tank heater).

2. Measuring element (thermometer).

3. Controller.

4. Final control element (variable transformer or control valve).

2.2. Block diagram of control systems

A good overall picture of the relationships among variables in the control system may be obtained by preparing a *block diagram.* It indicates the flow of information around the control system and the function of each part of the system.

Much more will be said about block diagrams later, but the reader can undoubtedly form a good intuitive notion about them by comparing Figure 2.1 with the physical description of the process.

Particularly significant is the fact that each component of the system is represented by a block, with little regard for the actual physical characteristics of the represented component (e.g., the tank or controller).

The major interest is in (1) the relationship between the signals entering and leaving the block and (2) the manner in which information flows around the system.

- **Closed loop:** The measured value of the controlled variable is fed back to the controller.
- **Controller:** A device that outputs a signal to the process or final control element based on the magnitude of the error signal. A proportional controller outputs a signal proportional to the error.
- **Deviation variable:** The difference between the actual value of a variable and its steady-state value. Block diagrams are *always* constructed using deviation variables.
- **Error:** The difference between the value of the set point and that of the measured variable.
- **Final control element:** A device that provides a modulated input to the process in response to a signal from the controller. For example, this may be a heater, a control valve, or a variety of other devices.

- **Load:** The change in any process variable that can cause the controlled variable to change.

- **Measuring element:** A sensor used to determine the value of the controlled variable and to send it to the comparator/controller. Examples include a thermocouple (temperature), a strain gage (pressure), a gas chromatograph (composition), and a pH electrode (acidity). These sensors typically have some dynamic behavior associated with them and can affect the design of the control system.

- **Regulator problem:** The goal of a control system for this type of problem is to enable the system to compensate for load changes and maintain the controlled variable at the set point.

- **Set point:** The desired value of the controlled variable.

2.3. On off controller

2.3.1. Principle of On off controller

- On-Off control is the simplest form of feedback control. An on-off controller simply drives the manipulated variable from fully closed to fully open depending on the position of the controlled variable relative to the set point.

- A common example of on-off control is the temperature control in a domestic heating system. When the temperature is below the thermostat set point the heating system is switched on and when the temperature is above the set point the heating switches off.

- There is, however, a bit of subtlety applied in practical on-off systems. If the heating switches on and off the instant the measured temperature crossed the set point then the system would *chatter* – repeatedly switch on and off at very high frequency.

- If this happened the boiler wouldn't last very long! To avoid chattering, practical on-off controllers usually have a *dead band* around the set point.

- When the measured value lies within this dead-band the controller does nothing – it's only when the value moves outside that action is taken.

- The effect of this is to introduce continuous oscillation in the value of the controlled variable – the large the dead-band the higher the amplitude and lower the frequency.

2.3.2. Example of On off controller

- The valve in the inflow line to the system is an electrically operated solenoid valve. (Remember an electrically operated solenoid valve has only two operating positions fully open or fully closed.)

- Assume that under initial conditions with a demand on the system the level will start to fall and V1 will have to be opened to provide an inflow. This can easily be achieved by mounting a differential pressure switch, P1 at the bottom of the tank to operate when the level falls to L1. When the level is at L1 the liquid will be height h1 above switch.

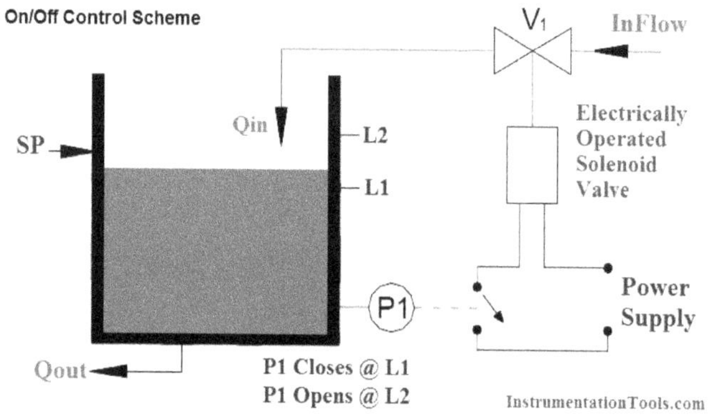

Figure2.2: ON/OFF Control system

The pressure at the switch will be **P1 = ρgh1.**

P = the mass density of the liquid

g = the acceleration due to gravity

h1 = the height of the liquid

- The resulting switch closure can energize the solenoid valve V1 causing an inflow to the tank.

Assuming the valve is correctly sized, this will cause a rise in the level back towards the set point.

- In order to arrest the rise in level the built in differential feature of the switch can be employed to de-energize the solenoid valve when level L2 is reached. This system will achieve a mean level in the tank about the desired set point. This method is known as ON/OFF control.

- Clearly it is impossible to maintain the system at the set point since there must be a difference in the operating levels L1 and L2 as the valve can only be energized or de-energized. It is often counter productive to try to reduce the differential between L1 and L2 to too small a value as this will result in excessive cycling, and hence wear, of the valve. Usual practice is to control with a dead band about the set point as shown in Figure 2.3.

- The sinusoidal cycling is typical of on/off control. On/off control can be used to advantage on a sluggish system, i.e., where the periodic time is large. Typical uses in electric heater controls, if fine control is required a simple on/off control system is inadequate.

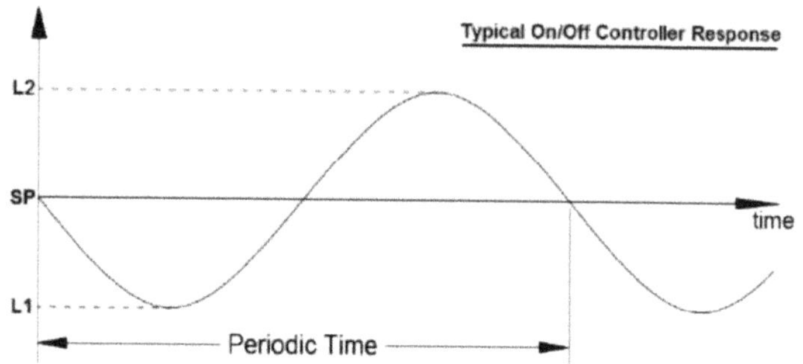

Figure 2.3: ON/OFF Controller Response

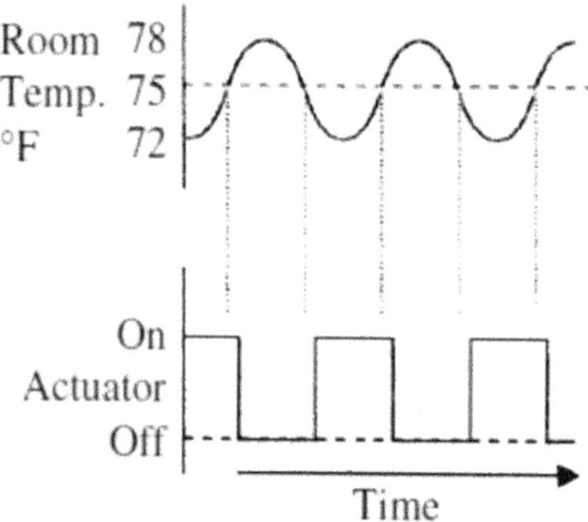

Figure 2.4: Room heating system with simple ON/OFF action of a room heating system

- Figure 2.4 shows an example of a simple room heating system. The top graph shows the room temperature or measured variable and the lower graph shows the actuator signal. The room temperature reference is set at 75°F.

- When the air is being heated, the temperature in the center of the room has already reached 77°F before the temperature at the sensor reaches the reference temperature of 75°F and similarly as the room cools, the temperature in the room will drop to 73°F before the temperature at the sensor reaches 75°F. Hence, the room temperature will go from about 72°F to 78°F due to the inertia in the system.

2.3.3. Differential action of On off controller

- Differential or delayed ON/OFF action is a mode of operation where the simple ON/OFF action has hysteresis or a dead-band built in. Figure 2.5 shows an example of a room heating system similar to that shown in Figure2.4 accept that instead of the thermostat turning ON and OFF at the set reference of 75°, the switching points are delayed by ±3°F.

- As can be seen in the top graph, the room temperature reaches 78°F before the thermostat turns OFF the actuator and the room temperature falls to 72°F before the actuator is turned ON giving a built in hysteresis of 6°F. There is, of course, still some inertia. Hence, the room temperature will go from about 70°F to about 80°F.

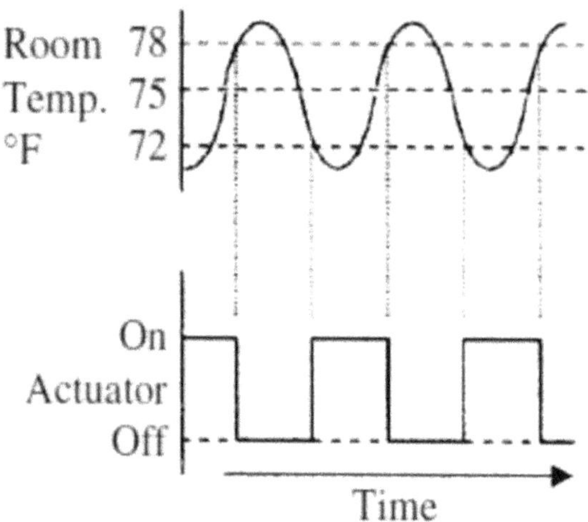

Figure 2.5: Room heating system with differential ON/OFF action

Following are a few aspects of On-Off Control that you should keep in mind when considering it for commercial application:

- **An Open or Shut Case**

As its name implies, On-Off Control assigns the Controller Output (CO) to one of two positions such that the final control element (FCE) is either fully open or fully closed. Unlike intermediate value or PID control, there is no in between. Most industrial processes require greater latitude when it comes to adjusting the CO as position.

- **Ups and Downs**

On-Off Control can result in excessive variability as the controller has so few options for maintaining Set Point. A process equipped with On-Off Control will constantly overshoot its Set Point and cycle as a result. The work demanded of the FCE regularly accelerates the time to failure and increases maintenance costs.

- **Setting Boundaries**

Dead band is a range of operation around the Set Point and within which the controller's action will not change. On-Off Control with Dead band establishes upper and lower boundaries that are acceptable to the control loops operation. While Dead bands cushion reduces wear on the FCE, variability remains within the process which can present challenges for other downstream processes.

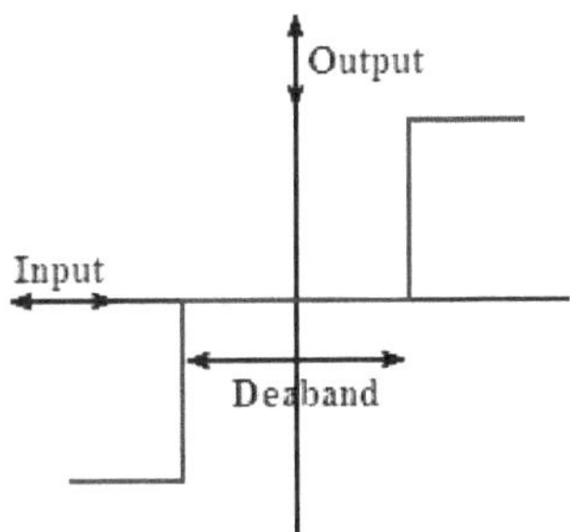

2.3.4. Summary of On off controller

- On/off control – control signal is either 0% or 100%.

- Control at set point not achievable, a dead band must be incorporated.

- Useful for large, sluggish systems particularly those incorporating electric heaters.

2.4. Proportional Integral Control (PI)

The most common of all continuous industrial process control action is proportional control action. The amplitude of the output variable from a process is measured and converted to an electrical signal.

This signal is compared to a set reference point. Any difference in amplitude between the two (error signal) is amplified and fed to a control valve (actuator) as a correction signal.

The control valve controls one of the inputs to the process. Changing this input will result in the output amplitude changing until it is equal to the set reference or the error signal is zero.

The amplitude of the correction signal is transmitted to the actuator controlling the input variable and is proportional to the percentage change in the output variable amplitude measured with respect to the set reference.

In industrial processing a different situation exists than with a room heating system. The industrial system has low inertia; overshoot and response times must be minimized for fast recovery and to keep processing tolerances within tight limits.

In order to achieve these goals fast reaction and settling times are needed. There may also be more than one variable to be controlled and more than one output being measured in a process.

- *Proportional plus Integral* (PI) action also known as reset action, was developed to correct for long-term loads and applies a correction proportional to the area under the change in the variable curve.

- Figure 2.6 gives some examples of the integration of a curve or the area under a curve. In the top example the area under the square wave increases rapidly but remains constant when the square wave drops back to zero.

- In the triangular section the area increases rapidly at the apex but increases slowly as the triangle approaches zero; when the triangle goes negative, the area reduces.

- In the lower example the area increases more rapidly when the sine wave is at its maximum and slower as it approaches the zero level.

- During the negative portion of the sine wave, the area is reduced. Proportional action gives a response to a change in the measured variable but does not fully correct the change in the measured variable due to its limited gain.

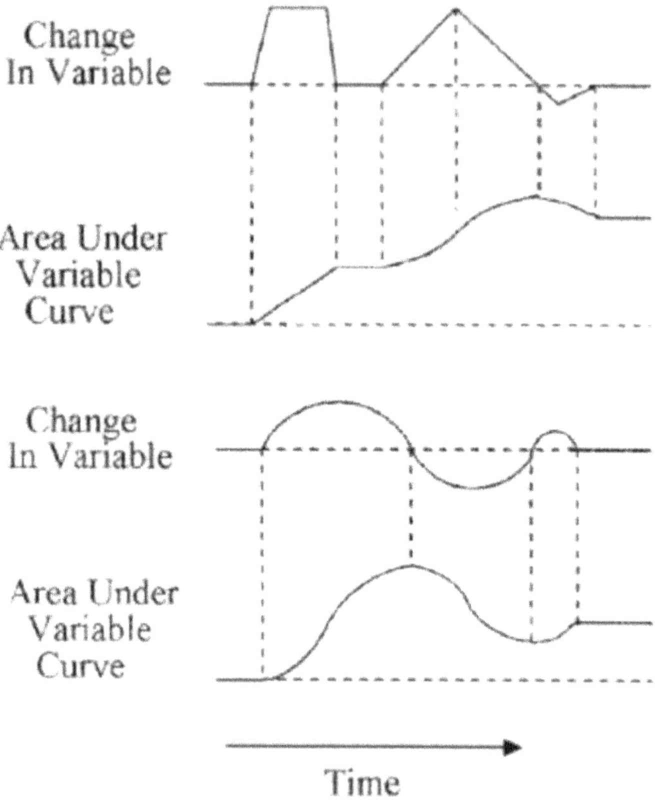

Figure 2.6: Proportional and integral action: variable change with area under the graph

- For instance, if the gain in the proportional amplifier is 100, then when a change in load occurs, 99 percent of the change is corrected. However, a 1 percent error signal is required for amplification to drive the actuator to change the manipulated variable.

- The 1 percent error signal is effectively an "offset" in the variable with respect to the reference. Integral action gives a slower response to changes in the measured variable to avoid overshoot, but has a high gain so that with long-term load changes it takes over control of the manipulated variable and applies the correction signal to the actuator.

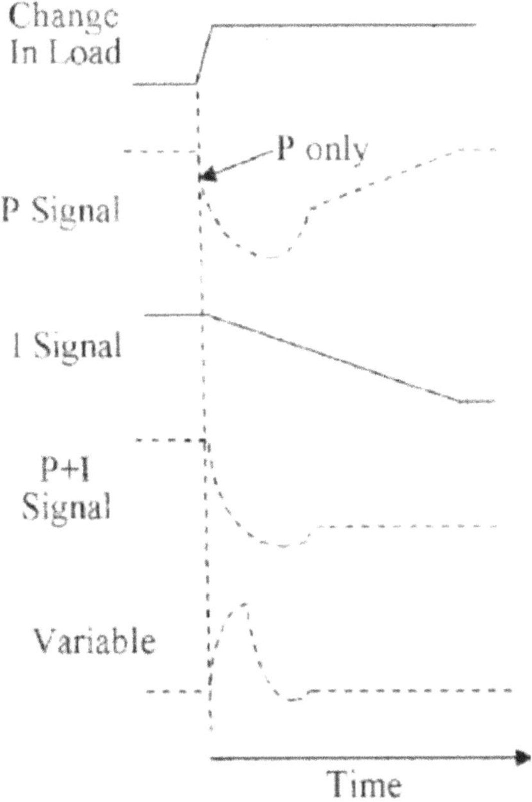

Figure 2.7: Proportional and integral action: effect of proportional and integral action on a variable

51

- Because of the returns the proportional amplifier to its normal operating point, so that it can correct for other fluctuations in the measured variable.

- Note that these corrections are done at relatively high speeds. The older pneumatic systems are much slower and can take several seconds to make such a correction.

- Figure 2.7 shows the PI corrective action waveforms. When a change in loading occurs, the P signal responds to take corrective action to restore the measured variable to its set point; simultaneously, the integral signal starts to change linearly to supply the long term correction, thus allowing the proportional signal to return to its normal operating point as is shown.

- Here again integral action can become complex and further discussion is considered to be outside the scope of this text.

2.5. Proportional Derivative Control (PD)

- *Proportional plus derivative* (PD) action was developed in an attempt to reduce the correction time that would have occurred using proportional action alone.

- Derivative action senses the rate of change of the measured variable and applies a correction signal that is proportional to the rate of change only (this is also called rate action or anticipatory action).

- Figure 2.8 shows some examples of derivative action. As can be seen in this example, a derivative output is obtained only when the load is changing.

- The derivative of a positive slope is a positive signal and the derivative of a negative slope is a negative signal; zero slopes give zero signals as shown.

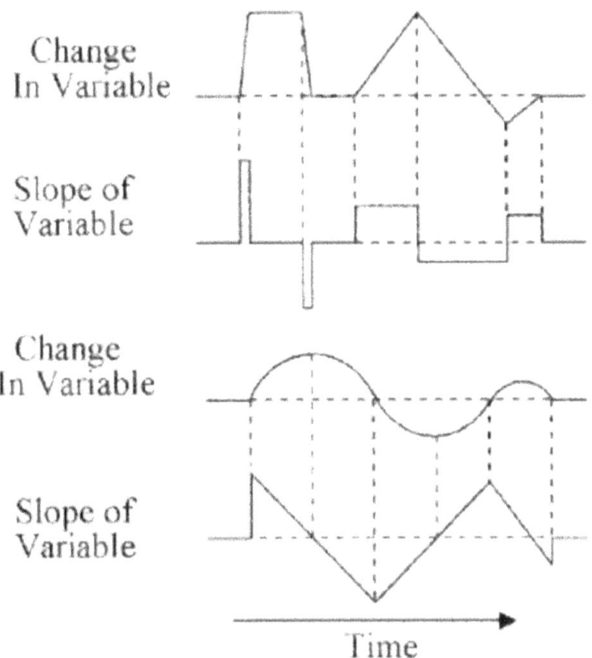

Figure 2.8: Proportional and derivative action: variable change with resulting slope

- Figure 2.9 shows the effect of PD action on the correction time. When a change in loading is sensed as shown, both the proportional and derivative signals are generated and added.

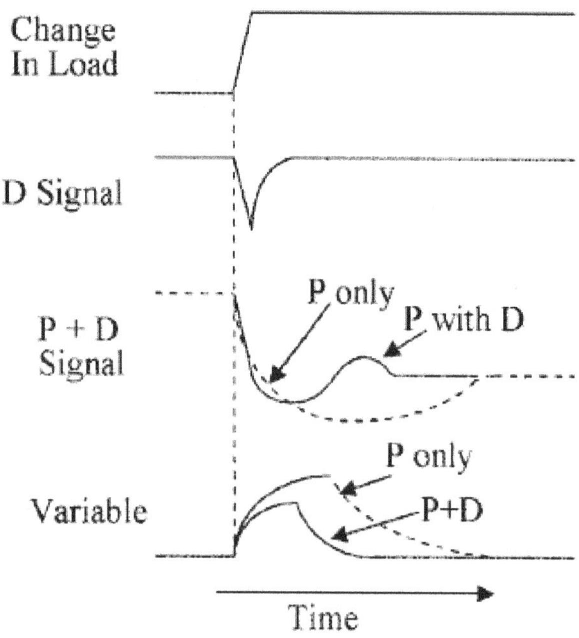

Figure 2.9: Proportional and derivative action: effect of proportional and derivative action on a variable

- The significance of combining these two signals is to produce a signal that speeds up the actuator's control signal. The faster reaction time of the control signal reduces the time to implement corrective action reducing the excursion of the measured variable and it's settling time.

- The amplitudes of these signals must be adjusted for optimum operation or overshoot or under shoot can still occur.

The change in output level may be a gradual change, a large on-demand change, or caused by a change in the reference level setting. An example of an on-demand change would be cleaning stations using hot water at a required fixed temperature, as shown in **Figure2.10**.

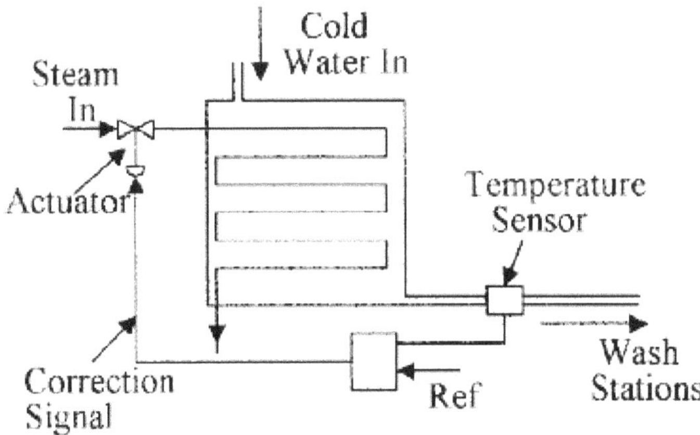

Figure 2.10: Water heater: showing a feedback loop for constant temperature output

At one point in time the demand could be very low with a low flow rate as would be the case if only one cleaning station were in use. If cleaning commenced at several of the other stations, the demand could increase in steps or there could be a sudden rise to a very high flow rate.

The increased flow rate would cause the water temperature to drop. The drop in water temperature would cause the temperature sensor to send a correction signal to the actuator controlling the steam flow, so as to increase the steam flow to raise the temperature of the water to bring it back to the set reference level (see Figure2.10). The rate of correction will depend on the inertia in the system, gain in the feedback loop, allowable amount of overshoot, and so forth.

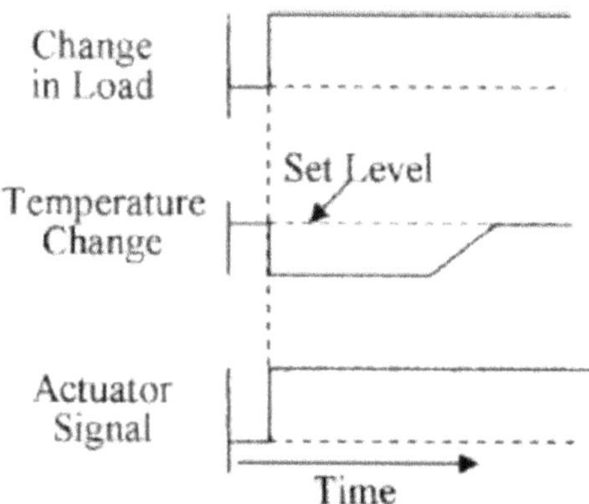

Figure 2.11: Water heater: effect of load changes on the temperature of the water from the water heater

In a closed loop feedback system settings are critical. If the system has too much gain, i.e., the amplitude of the correction signal is too great, it will cause the controlled variable to over correct for the error, which in turn will give a false error signal in the reverse direction.

The actuator will then try to correct for the false error signal. This can, in turn, send a larger correction signal to the actuator, which will cause the system to oscillate or cause an excessively long settling or lag time. If the gain in the system is too low the correction signal is too small and the correction will never be fully completed, or again an excessive amount of time is taken for the output to reach the set reference level.

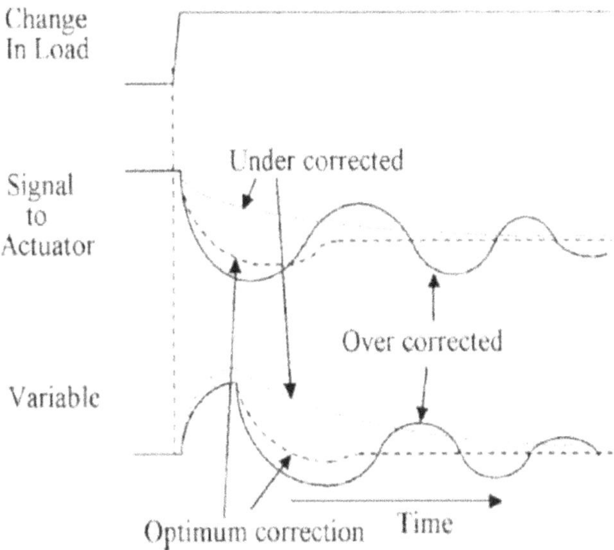

Figure 2.12: Effect of loop gain on correction time using proportional action with over correction and under correction

This effect is shown in Figure2.11, as can be seen in comparing the over corrected (excessive gain) and the under corrected (too little gain) to the optimum gain case (with just a little overshoot). The variable takes a much longer time for the correction to be implemented than in the optimum case. In many processes this long delay or lag time is unacceptable.

2.6. Proportional Integral Derivative Control (PID)

- A combination of all three of the actions is more commonly referred to as PID action. The waveforms of PID action are illustrated in **Figure2.13**.

- PID is the most often used corrective action for process control. There are however, many other types of control actions based upon PID action.

- Understanding the fundamentals of PID action gives a good foundation for understanding other types of controllers.

- The waveforms used have been idealized for ease of the explanation and are only an example of what may be encountered in practice.

- Loading is a function of demand and is not affected by the control functions or actions; the control function is to ensure that the variables are within their specified limits.

- To give an approximate indication of the use of PID controllers for different types of loops, the following are general rules that should be followed:

✓ Pressure control requires proportional and integral; derivative is normally not required.

✓ Level control uses proportional and sometimes integral, derivative is not normally required.

✓ Flow control requires proportional and integral; derivative is not normally required.

✓ Temperature control uses proportional, integral, and derivative usually with integral set for a long time period.

- However, the above are general rules and each application has its own requirements.

- Typical feedback loops have been discussed. The reader should, however, be aware that there are other kinds of control loops used in process control such as cascade, ratio, and feed-forward.

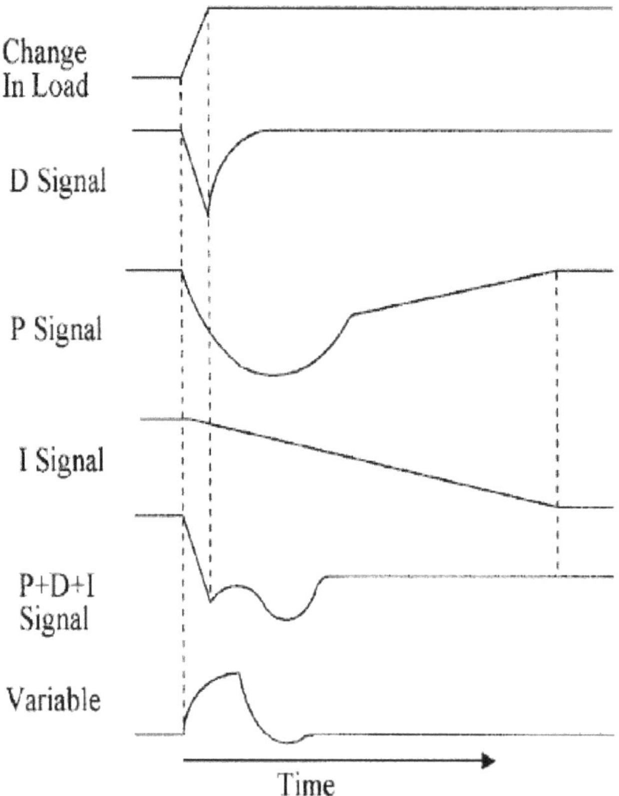

Figure 2.13: Waveforms for proportional plus integral action and waveforms for proportional plus derivative and integral action

2.7. PID electronic controller

Figure 2.14 shows the block diagram of an analog PID controller. The measured variable from the sensor is compared to the set point in the first unity gain comparator;

its output is the difference between the two signals or the error signal.

This signal is fed to the integrator via an inverting unity gain buffer and to the proportional amplifier and differentiator via a second inverting unity gain comparator, which compares the error signal to the integrator output. Initially, with no error signal the output of the integrator is zero so that the zero error signals are also present at the output of the second comparator.

When there is a change in the measured variable, the error signal is passed through the second comparator to the proportional amplifier and the differentiator where it is amplified in the proportional amplifier, added to the differential signal in a summing circuit, and fed to the actuator to change the input variable. Although the integrator sees the error signal, it is slow to react and so its output does not change immediately, but starts to integrate the error signal.

If the error signal is present for an extended period of time, the integrator will supply the correction signal via the summing circuit to the actuator and input the correction signal to the second comparator.

This will reduce the effective error signal to the proportional amplifier to zero, when the integrator is supplying the full correction signal to the actuator. Any new change in the error signal will still be passed through the second comparator as the integrator is only supplying an offset to correct for the first long-term error signal. The proportional and differential amplifiers can then correct for any new changes in the error signal.

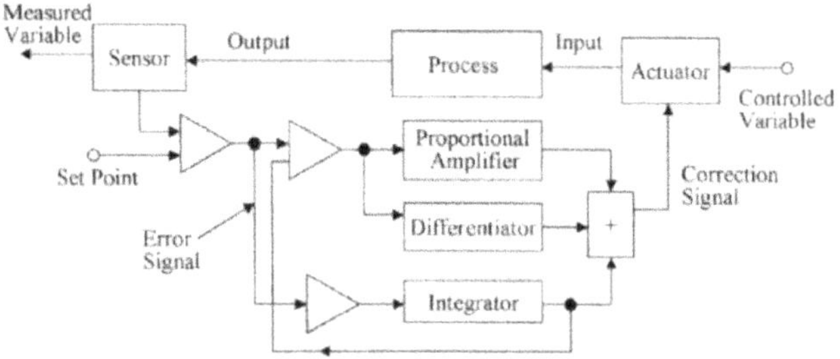

Figure 2.14: Block schematic of a PID electronic controller

2.8. Control Valves and its Characteristics

- The control valve is essentially a variable resistance to the flow of a fluid, in which the resistance and therefore the flow can be changed by a signal from a process controller.

- The control valve consists of an actuator and a valve. The valve itself is divided into the body and the trim. The body consists of housing for mounting the actuator and connections for attachment of the valve to a supply line and a delivery line.

- The trim, which is enclosed within the body, consists of a plug, a valve seat, and a valve stem. The actuator moves the valve stem as the pressure on a spring-loaded diaphragm changes. The stem moves a plug in a valve seat in order to change the resistance to flow through the valve.

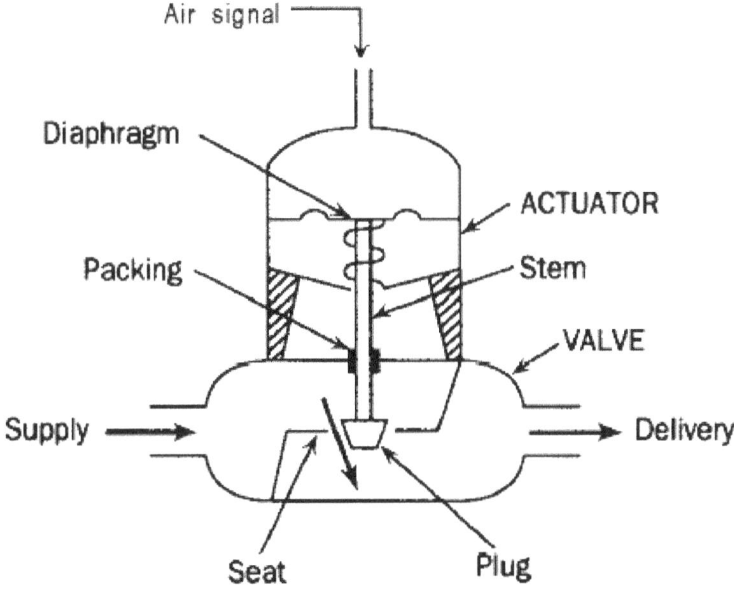

Figure 2.15: Pressure-to-close valve with single seating

- When a valve is supplied by the manufacturer, the actuator and the valve are attached to each other to form one unit.

- The selection of control valves for a particular application depends on many variables; such as the corrosive nature of the fluid, temperature of operation, pressures involved, high or low flow velocities, volume of flow, and the amount of suspended solids.

- Valves are the final element in a control loop and are critical in providing the correct flow for process control.

- The valve is subject to operation in very harsh conditions and one of the most costly elements in the process control system.

- The choice and correct installation requires both knowledge and experience. Careful attention must be paid to the system requirements and manufacturers' specifications, only then can a careful valve selection be made.

- **Some of the factors affecting the choice of valves are as follows:**

1. Type of valve for two-way or three-way fail-safe considerations, and so on.

2. Valve size from flow requirements; care must be taken to avoid both oversizing and under sizing.

3. Materials used in the valve construction, considering pressure, size, and corrosion. Materials used in valves range from PVC to brass to steel.

4. Tightness of shutoff: Valves are classified by quality of shutoff by leakage at maximum pressure. Valves are classified into six classes depending on leakage from 0.5 percent of rated capacity to 0.15 mL/min. for a 1-in dia. valve.

5. Acceptable pressure drop across the valve.

6. Valve body for linear or rotary motion, i.e., globe, diaphragm versus ball, butterfly, and so forth.

- The type of valve or plug depends on the nature of the process reaction. In the case of a fast reaction with small load changes, control is only slightly affected by valve characteristics.

- When the process is slow with large load changes, valve characteristics are important, i.e., if the load change is linear, a valve with a linear characteristic should be used, in the case of a nonlinear load change, a valve with an equal percentage change may be required.

2.9. Valve sizing

In order to specify the size of a valve in terms of its capacity to provide flow when fully open, the following equation is used:

$$q = C_v \sqrt{\frac{\Delta p_v}{G}}$$

$$(2.1)$$

Where

q = flow rate, gpm

$\Delta \mathbf{p_v}$ = pressure drop across the wide-open valve, psi

G = specific gravity of fluid at stream temperature relative to water; for water G = 1.

C_v = factor associated with capacity of valve

2.10. Valve characteristics

- The function of a control valve is to vary the flow of fluid through the valve by means of a change of pressure to the valve top.

- The relation between the flow through the valve and the valve stem position (or lift) is called the valve characteristic, which can be conveniently described by means of a graph as shown in Figure 2.16 where three types of characteristics are illustrated.

- In general, the flow through a control valve for a specific fluid at a given temperature can be expressed as: $q = f_1(L, P_0, P_1)$

Where q = volumetric flow rate, L = valve stem position (or lift), P_0 = upstream pressure and P_1 = downstream pressure

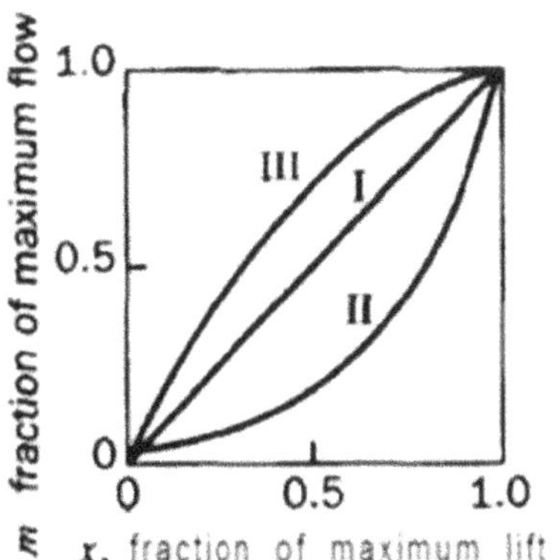

FIGURE 2.16: Inherent valve characteristics (pressure drop across valve is constant) I linear, II increasing sensitivity (e.g. equal percentage valve), III decreasing sensitivity

- The inherent valve characteristic is determined fixed values of pa and p_1, for which case, $q = f_1(L, P_0, P_1)$ which becomes: $q = f_2(L)$

- The types of valve characteristics can be defined in terms of the sensitivity of the valve, which is simply the fractional change in flow to the fractional change in stem position for fixed upstream and downstream pressures.

- In terms of valve characteristics, valves can be divided into three types: decreasing sensitivity, linear, and increasing sensitivity. These types are shown in Figure 2.16, where the fractional flow m is plotted against fractional lift x.

- For the decreasing sensitivity type, the sensitivity (or slope) decreases with m. For the linear type, the sensitivity is constant and the characteristic curve is a straight line. For the increasing sensitivity type, the sensitivity increases with flow.

- Valve characteristic curves, such as the ones shown in Figure 216, can be obtained experimentally for any valve by measuring the flow through the valve as a function of lift (or valve-top pressure) under conditions of constant upstream and downstream pressures.

- Two types of valves that are widely used are the linear valve and the logarithmic (or equal percentage) valve. The linear valve is one for which the sensitivity is constant and the relation between flow and lift is linear. The equal percentage valve is of the increasing sensitivity type.

Chapter 3

Transfer function of Control system

3.1. Transfer function of Proportional control

- The simplest type of controller is the proportional controller. (The ON/OFF control is really the simplest, but it is a special case of the proportional controller as we'll see shortly.)

- Our goal is to reduce the error between the process output and the set point. The proportional controller, as we will see, can reduce the error, but cannot eliminate it.

- If we can accept some residual error, proportional control may be the proper choice for the situation.

- The proportional controller has only one adjustable parameter, the controller gain.

- The proportional controller produces an output signal (pressure in the case of a pneumatic controller, current, or voltage for an electronic controller) that is proportional to the error ε.

This action may be expressed as

$$p = K_c \varepsilon + p_s \tag{3.1}$$

Where

p = output signal from controller, psig or mA

Kc = proportional gain, or sensitivity

ε = error = (set point) - (measured variable)

p_s = a constant, the steady-state output from the controller

- The error ε, which is the difference between the set point and the signal from the measuring element, may be in any suitable units. However, the units of the set point and the measured variable must be the same, since the error is the difference between these quantities.

- In a controller having adjustable gain, the value of the gain K c can be varied by entering it into the controller, usually by means of a keypad (or a knob on older equipment).

- The value of p s is the value of the output signal when ε is zero, and in most controllers p s can be adjusted to obtain the required output signal when the control system is at steady state and $\varepsilon = 0$.

To obtain the transfer function of Eq. (3.1), we first introduce the deviation variable

$$P = p - p_s \tag{3.2}$$

into Eq. (3.1). At time t = 0, we assume the error ε s to be zero. Then e is already a deviation variable. Equation (3.1) becomes

P (t) = K$_c$ ε (t) (3.3)

Taking the transform of Eq. (3.3) gives the transfer function of an ideal proportional controller.

Proportional controller transfer function

$$\frac{P(s)}{\varepsilon(s)} = K_c$$

(3.4)

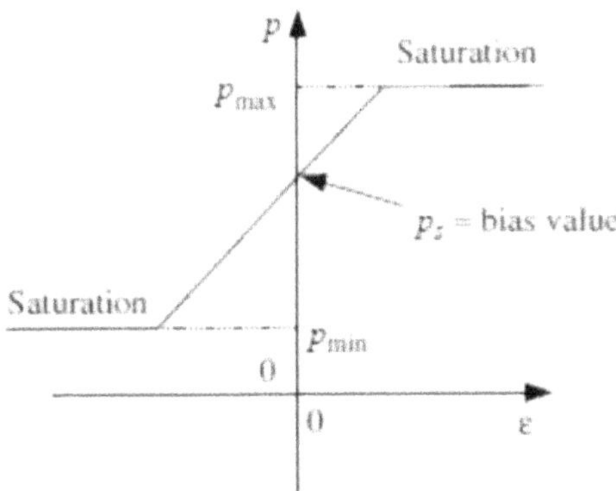

FIGURE 3.1: Proportional controller output as a function of error input to the controller: Ideal behavior

FIGURE 3.2: Proportional controller output as a function of error input to the controller: actual behavior

The actual behavior of a proportional controller is depicted in Figure 3.1 and 3.2. The controller output will saturate (level out) at p_{max} = 15 psig or 20 mA at the upper end and at p_{min} = 3 psig or 4 mA at the lower end of the output. The ideal transfer function Eq. (3.4) does not predict this saturation phenomenon.

3.2. Transfer function of Proportional-integral (PI) control

- If we cannot tolerate any residual error, we will have to introduce an additional control mode: integral control.

- If we add integral control to our proportional controller, we have what is termed PI, or proportional-integral control.

- The integral mode ultimately drives the error to zero. This controller has two adjustable parameters for which we select values, the gain and the integral time. Thus it is a bit more complicated than a proportional controller, but in exchange for the additional complexity, we reap the advantage of no error at steady state.

- PI control is described by the relationship

$$p = K_c \varepsilon + \frac{K_c}{t_I} \int_0^t \varepsilon \, dt + p_s \tag{3.5}$$

Where

K_c = proportional gain

t_I = integral time, min

p_s = constant (the bias value)

- In this case, we have added to the proportional action term $K_c \varepsilon$ another term that is proportional to the integral of the error.

- The values of K_c and t_I are both adjustable.

- To visualize the response of this controller, consider the response to a unit-step change in error, as shown in Figure 3.3.

- This unit-step response is most directly obtained by inserting $\varepsilon = 1$ into Eq. (3.5), which yields

$$p(t) = K_c + \frac{K_c}{t_I} t + p_s \tag{3.6}$$

- Notice that p changes suddenly by an amount K c and then changes linearly with time at a rate K_c / t_I.

- To obtain the transfer function of Eq. (3.5), we again introduce the deviation variable $P = p - p_s$ into Eq. (3.5) and then take the transform to obtain Proportional-integral controller transfer function

$$\frac{P(s)}{\mathcal{E}(s)} = K_c\left(1 + \frac{1}{\tau_I s}\right)$$

(3.7)

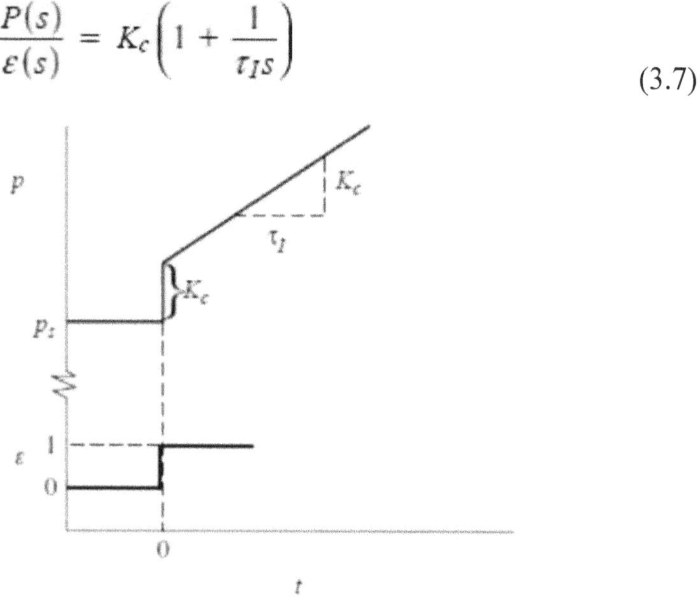

FIGURE 3.3: Response of a PI controller to a unit-step change in error

- Some manufacturers prefer to use the term reset rate, which is defined as the reciprocal of t_I.

- The integral adjustment on a controller may be denoted by integral time or reset rate (carefully check the specific controller to be sure which value to enter).

- The calibration of the proportional and integral action is often checked by observing the jump and slope of a step response, as shown in Figure 3.3.

3.3. Transfer function of Proportional-derivative (PD) control

- Derivative control is another mode that can be added to our proportional or proportional-integral controllers.
- It acts upon the derivative of the error, so it is most active when the error is changing rapidly.
- It serves to reduce process oscillations.

This mode of control may be represented by

$$p = K_c \varepsilon + K_c \tau_D \frac{d\varepsilon}{dt} + p_s \tag{3.8}$$

Where K_c = proportional gain

ζ_D = derivative time, min

p_s = constant (bias value)

- In this case, we have added to the proportional term another term $K_c \zeta_D \, de/dt$, which is proportional to the derivative of the error.
- The values of K_c and ζ_D are both adjustable. Other terms that are used to describe the derivative action are rate control and anticipatory control.
- The action of this controller can be visualized by considering the response to a linear change in error as shown in Figure 3.4.

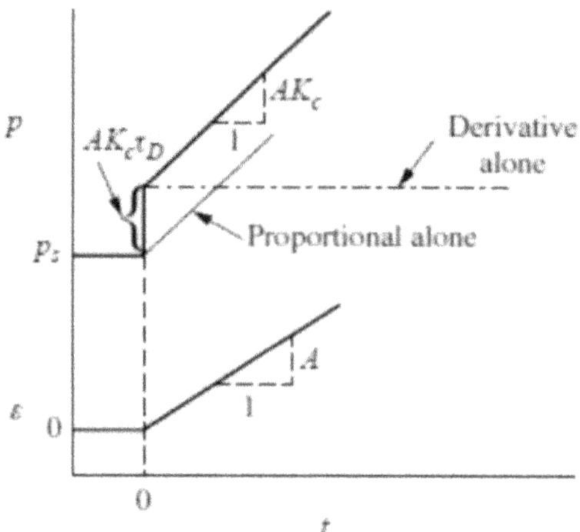

FIGURE 3.4: Response of a PD controller to a ramp input in error

This response is obtained by introducing the linear function $\varepsilon(t) = At$ into Eq. (1) to obtain

$$p(t) = AK_c t + AK_c \tau_D + p_s$$

$$(3.9)$$

- Notice that p changes suddenly by an amount $A K_c \zeta_D$ as a result of the derivative action and then changes linearly at a rate $A K_c$.

- The effect of derivative action in this case is to anticipate the linear change in error by adding output $A K_c \zeta_D$ to the proportional action.

- The controller is taking pre-emptive action to counter the anticipated change in the error that it predicted from the slope of the error versus time curve.

- To obtain the transfer function from Eq. (3.8), we introduce the deviation variable

P = p - p$_s$ and then take the transform to obtain,

Proportional-derivative controller transfer function

$$\frac{P(s)}{\varepsilon(s)} = K_c(1 + \tau_D s)$$

(3.10)

3.4. Transfer function of Proportional-integral-derivative (PID) control

This mode of control is a combination of the previous modes and is given by the expression Proportional-integral-derivative Controller.

$$p = K_c \varepsilon + K_c \tau_D \frac{d\varepsilon}{dt} + \frac{K_c}{\tau_I} \int_0^t \varepsilon \, dt + p_s$$

(3.11)

- In this case, all three values K_c , ζ_D , and ζ_I can be adjusted in the controller.
- The transfer function for this controller can be obtained from the Laplace transform of Eq. (3.11); thus Proportional-integral-derivative controller transfer function

$$\frac{P(s)}{\varepsilon(s)} = K_c\left(1 + \tau_D s + \frac{1}{\tau_I s}\right)$$

(3.12)

Derivative action is based on how rapidly the error is changing, not the magnitude of the error or how long the error has persisted. It is based on the slope of the error versus time curve at any instant in time.

Therefore, a rapidly changing error signal will induce a large derivative response. "Noisy" error signals because significant problems for derivative action because of the rapidly changing slope of the error caused by noise.

Derivative control should be avoided in these situations unless the error signal can be filtered to remove the noise.

3.5. Motivation for Addition of Integral and Derivative Control Modes

Having introduced ideal transfer functions for integral and derivative modes of control, we now wish to indicate the practical motivation for use of these modes. The curves of Figure 3.5 show the behavior of a typical feedback control system using different kinds of control when it is subjected to a permanent disturbance.

This may be visualized in terms of the stirred-tank temperature control system. The value of the controlled variable is seen to rise at time zero owing to the disturbance. With no control, this variable continues to rise to a new steady-state value. With control, after some time the control system begins to take action to try to maintain the controlled variable close to the value that existed before the disturbance occurred.

With proportional action only, the control system is able to arrest the rise of the controlled variable and ultimately bring it to rest at a new steady-state value. The difference between this new steady-state value and the original value (the set point, in this case) is called offset.

For the particular system shown, the offset is seen to be only about 20 percent of the ultimate change that would have been realized for this disturbance in the absence of control.

As shown by the PI curve, the addition of integral action eliminates the offset; the controlled variable ultimately returns to the original value. This advantage of integral action is balanced by the disadvantage of a more oscillatory behavior.

The addition of derivative action to the PI action gives a definite improvement in the response. The rise of the controlled variable is arrested more quickly, and it is returned rapidly to the original value with little or no oscillation.

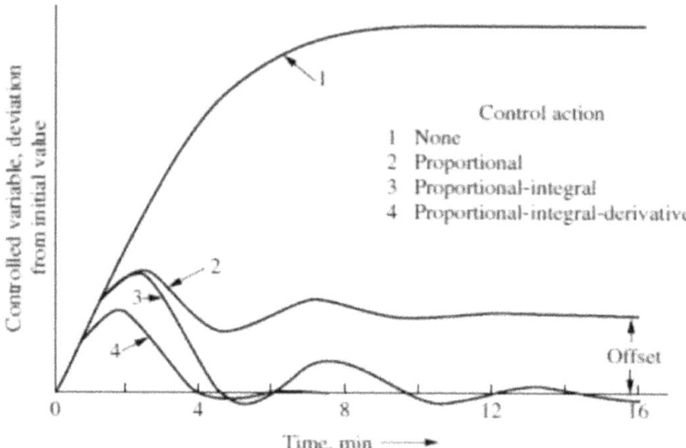

FIGURE 3.5: Response of a typical control system showing the effects of various modes of control

The selection among the control systems whose responses are shown in Figure 3.5 depends on the particular application.

- If an offset of about 20 percent is tolerable, proportional action would likely be selected.

- If no offset were tolerable, integral action would be added.

- If excessive oscillations had to be eliminated, derivative action might be added.

- The addition of each mode means, as we will see in later chapters, more difficult controller adjustment.

Our goal in forthcoming chapters will be to present the material that will enable the reader to develop curves such as those of Figure 3.5 and thereby to design efficient, economic control systems.

3.6. Block diagram of chemical reactor control system

To tie together the principles developed thus far and to illustrate further the procedure for reduction of a physical control system to a block diagram, we consider the two-tank chemical-reactor control system of Figure 3.6. This entire chapter serves as an example and may be omitted by the reader with no loss in continuity.

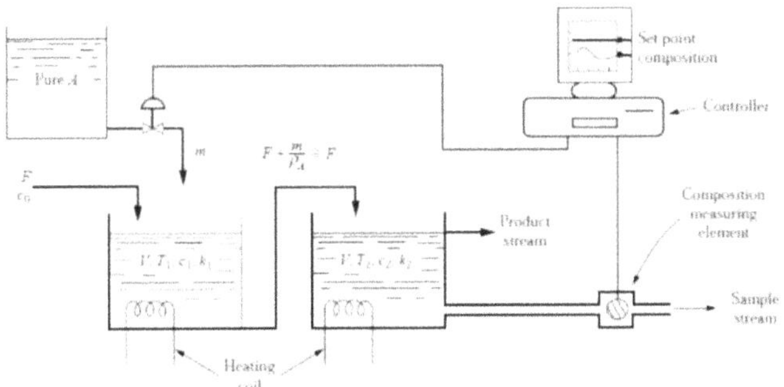

FIGURE 3.6: Control of a stirred-tank chemical reactor

A liquid stream enters tank 1 at a volumetric flow rate F cfm and contains reactant A at a concentration of c_0 mol A /ft^3. Reactant A decomposes in the tanks according to the irreversible chemical reaction

$$A \rightarrow B \tag{3.13}$$

The reaction is first-order and proceeds at a rate

$$r_A = -kc \tag{3.14}$$

Where

r_A = rate of formation of A, (mol A)/(ft^3·time)

c = concentration of A, mol A /ft^3

k = reaction rate constant (a function of temperature), time^{-1}

($k_1 \equiv$ tank 1, $k_2 \equiv$ tank 2)

The reaction is to be carried out in a series of two continuous stirred-tank reactors. The tanks are maintained at different temperatures. The temperature in tank 2 is to be greater than the temperature in tank 1, with the result that k_2, the reaction rate constant in tank 2, is greater than that in tank 1, k_1. We will neglect any changes in physical properties due to chemical reaction.

The purpose of the control system is to maintain c_2, the concentration of A leaving tank 2, at some desired value in spite of variations in the inlet concentration c_0. This will be accomplished by adding a stream of pure A to tank 1 through a control valve. We wish to produce a block diagram for the process so that we can simulate its response to changes in inlet concentration.

We have now completed the analysis of each component of the control system and have obtained a transfer function for each. These transfer functions can now be combined so that the overall system is represented by the block diagram in Figure 3.7.

In Figure 3.7, a block containing the transfer function $\mathbf{K_m}$ is placed at the positive inlet of the comparator in order to relate the set point in concentration units to a pneumatic signal, which matches the units of the feedback signal **B**.

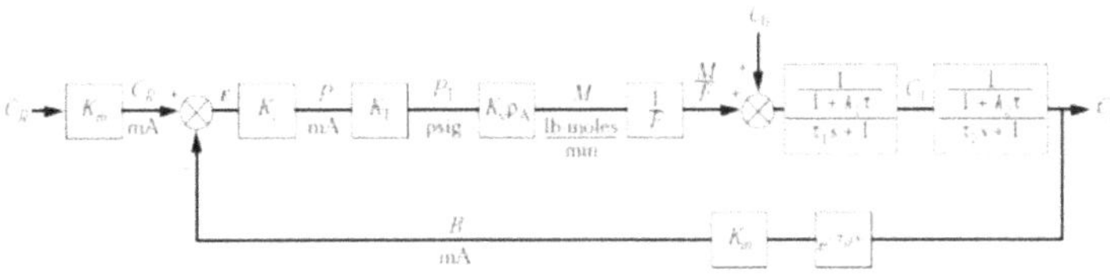

FIGURE 3.7: Block diagram for a chemical-reactor control system

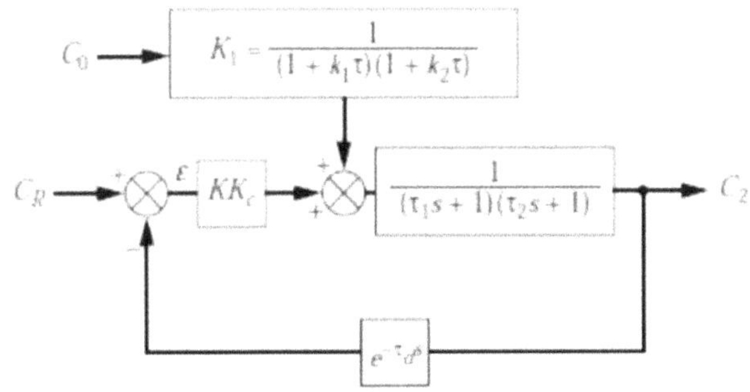

$$\tau_1 = 2, \ \tau_2 = 1, \ \tau_d = 0.5, \ K_1 = \frac{1}{4.5}$$

(3.15)

$$\text{Open-loop gain} = KK_c = \frac{K_m K_T K_1 \rho_A}{F(1 + k_1 \tau)(1 + k_2 \tau)} \quad K_c = 0.09 \, K_c$$

(3.16)

FIGURE 3.8: Equivalent block diagram for a chemical-reactor control system (C_R is now in concentration units)

If the pneumatic controller in Figure 3.7 were replaced by an electronic or computer based controller, the block for the controller in Figure 3.7 would be replaced by two blocks; one for the electronic controller and one for the converter, which converts the controller output (ma) to the pneumatic signal (psig). An equivalent diagram is shown in Figure 3.8 in which some of the blocks have been combined.

Numerical quantities for the parameters in the transfer functions are given in Figure 3.8. It should be emphasized that the block diagram is written for deviation variables. The true steady-state values, which are not given by the diagram, must be obtained from the analysis of the problem.

The example analyzed in this section will be used later in discussion of control system design. The design problem will be to select a value of K_c that gives satisfactory control of the composition C_2 despite the rather long transportation lag involved in getting information to the controller. In addition, we shall want to consider possible use of other modes of control for the system.

3.7. Concept of stability

The overall response of the control system was no higher than second-order. For these systems, the step response must resemble. Hence, the system is inherently stable. In this section we consider the problem of stability in a control system (Fig**ure 3.9**) only slightly more complicated than any studied previously.

This system might represent proportional control of two stirred-tank heaters with measuring lag. In this discussion, only set point changes are to be considered.

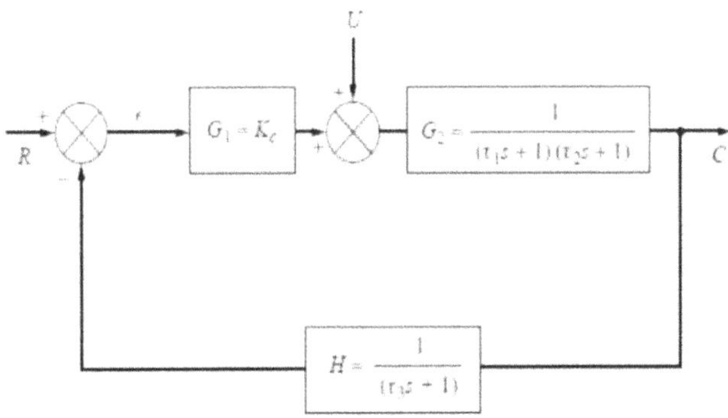

FIGURE: 3.9 Third-order control systems

$$\frac{C}{R} = \frac{G_1 G_2}{1 + G_1 G_2 H}$$

(3.17)

In terms of the particular transfer functions shown in Figure 3.9, C / R becomes, after some rearrangement,

$$\frac{C}{R} = \frac{K_c(\tau_3 s + 1)}{(\tau_1 s + 1)(\tau_2 s + 1)(\tau_3 s + 1) + K_c} \tag{3.18}$$

The denominator of Eq. (3.18) is a third-order polynomial. For a unit-step change in R, the transform of the response is

$$C = \frac{1}{s}\frac{K_c(\tau_3 s + 1)}{(\tau_1 s + 1)(\tau_2 s + 1)(\tau_3 s + 1) + K_c} \tag{3.19}$$

Definition of stability (Linear systems)

For our purposes, a stable system will be defined as one for which the output response is bounded for all bounded inputs. A system exhibiting an unbounded response to a bounded input is unstable.

This definition, although somewhat loose, is adequate for most of the linear systems and simple inputs that we shall study.

STABLE SYSTEM $\rightarrow$ a bounded input produces a bounded output (BIBO)

A bounded input function is a function of time that always falls within certain bounds during the course of time.

- For example, the step function and sinusoidal function are bounded inputs. The function $f(t) = t$ is obviously unbounded.

Although the definition of an unstable system states that the output becomes unbounded, this is true only in the mathematical sense. An actual physical system always exhibits bounds or constraints.

A linear mathematical model (set of linear differential equations describing the system) from which stability information is obtained is meaningful only over a certain range of variables.

- For example, a linear control valve gives a linear relation between flow and valve-top pressure only over the range of pressure (or flow) corresponding to values between which the valve is shut tight or wide open.

When the valve is wide open, for example, further change in pressure to the diaphragm will not increase the flow. We often describe such a limitation by the term saturation. A physical system, when unstable, may not follow the response of its linear mathematical model beyond certain physical bounds but rather may saturate.

However, the prediction of stability by the linear model is of utmost importance in a real control system since operation with the valve shut tight or wide open is clearly unsatisfactory control.

✓ **Therefore, the definition of stability for linear systems may be translated to the following criterion: A linear control system is unstable if any roots of its characteristic equation are on, or to the right of, the imaginary axis. Otherwise the system is stable.**

3.8. Routh test for stability

The Routh test is a purely algebraic method for determining how many roots of the characteristic equation have positive real parts; from this it can also be determined whether the system is stable, for if there are no roots with positive real parts, the system is stable.

The test is limited to systems that have polynomial characteristic equations. This means that it cannot be used to test the stability of a control system containing a transportation lag. The procedure for application of the Routh test is presented without proof.

The proof is available elsewhere (Routh, 1905) and is mathematically beyond the scope of this text. The procedure for examining the roots is to write the characteristic equation in the form

$$a_0 s^n + a_1 s^{n-1} + a_2 s^{n-2} + \cdots + a_n = 0$$

$$(3.20)$$

Where, a_0 is positive.

- (If a_0 is originally negative, both sides are multiplied by -1.) In this form, it is necessary that all the coefficients be positive if all the roots are to lie in the left half-plane.

$$a_0, a_1, a_2, .. , a_{n-1}, a_n \tag{3.21}$$

- If any coefficient is negative, the system is definitely unstable, and the Routh test is not needed to answer the question of stability. (However, in this case, the Routh test will tell us the number of roots in the right half-plane.)

- If all the coefficients are positive, the system may be stable or unstable. It is then necessary to apply the following procedure to determine stability.

Routh Array

Arrange the coefficients of Eq. (3.20) into the first two rows of the Routh array as follows:

Row				
1	a_0	a_2	a_4	a_6
2	a_1	a_3	a_5	a_7
3	b_1	b_2	b_3	
4	c_1	c_2	c_3	
5	d_1	d_2		
6	e_1	e_2		
7	f_1			
$n + 1$	g_1			

The array has been filled in for $n = 7$ to simplify the discussion. For any other value of n, the array is prepared in the same manner. In general, there are $n + 1$ rows. For n even, the first row has one more element than the second row.

The elements in the remaining rows are found from the formulas

$$b_1 = \frac{a_1 a_2 - a_0 a_3}{a_1} \tag{3.22}$$

$$b_2 = \frac{a_1 a_4 - a_0 a_5}{a_1} \quad \cdots \tag{3.23}$$

$$c_1 = \frac{b_1 a_3 - a_1 b_2}{b_1} \tag{3.24}$$

$$c_2 = \frac{b_1 a_5 - a_1 b_3}{b_1} \quad \cdots \tag{3.25}$$

The elements for the other rows are found from formulas that correspond to those just given. The elements in any row are always derived from the elements of the two preceding rows.

During the computation of the Routh array, any row can be divided by a positive constant without changing the results of the test. (The application of this rule often simplifies the arithmetic.)

Having obtained the Routh array, we can apply the following theorems to determine stability.

Theorems of the Routh test

Theorem 1

The necessary and sufficient condition for all the roots of the characteristic equation [Eq. (4)] to have negative real parts (stable system) is that all elements of the first column of the Routh array (a_0 , a_1 , b_1 , c_1 , etc.) be positive and nonzero.

Theorem 2

If some of the elements in the first column are negative, the number of roots with a positive real part (in the right half-plane) is equal to the number of sign changes in the first column.

Theorem 3

If one pair of roots is on the imaginary axis, equidistant from the origin and all other roots are in the left half-plane, then all the elements of the nth row will vanish and none of the elements of the preceding row will vanish. The location of the pair of imaginary roots can be found by solving the equation

$$Cs^2 + D = 0 \tag{3.26}$$

Where the coefficients C and D are the elements of the array in the $(n-1)^{st}$ row as read from left to right, respectively.

- The algebraic method for determining stability is limited in its usefulness in that all we can learn from it is whether a system is stable. It does not give us any idea of the degree of stability or the roots of the characteristic equation.

3.9. Piping & Instrumentations (P&I) diagram

- Piping and instrumentation diagrams (P&IDs) are used by the chemical process industry to document the control systems for their processes.

- The Instrument Society of America (ISA) produces a standards document [ISA-5.1-1984-(R1992)] "Instrument Symbols and Identification" that establishes a uniform means of designating instruments, control systems, and sensors used for measurement and control in a process.

- The standard is suitable for use in the chemical, petroleum, power generation, air conditioning, metal refining, and numerous other process industries.

- Table 3.1 shows some common conventions used for identifying process instrumentation and control on process drawings.

- Figure 3.10 shows an example of a level control loop for a process tank. The operation is as follows. The tank level is measured using a sensor, perhaps a differential pressure cell, indicated by the bubble containing LE on the diagram.

- The sensor is connected to a level transmitter, LT that sends an electrical signal (4 to 20 mA) to a level indicating controller LIC. Level alarms high and low, LAH and LAL, "monitor" the signal from the level transmitter and indicate an alarm situation if necessary.

- Notice from the symbols (the line through the bubble) that LIC, LAH, and LAL are all located in the control room, while LE and LT are mounted in the field. The level indicating controller determines the necessary signal to send to the valve, based on the current level in the tank, the set point, and the selected control algorithm being used (P or PID, for example).

- LY computes the necessary control air pressure signal (3 to 15 psig) to send to the level control valve LCV to properly respond to the controller output signal from LIC.

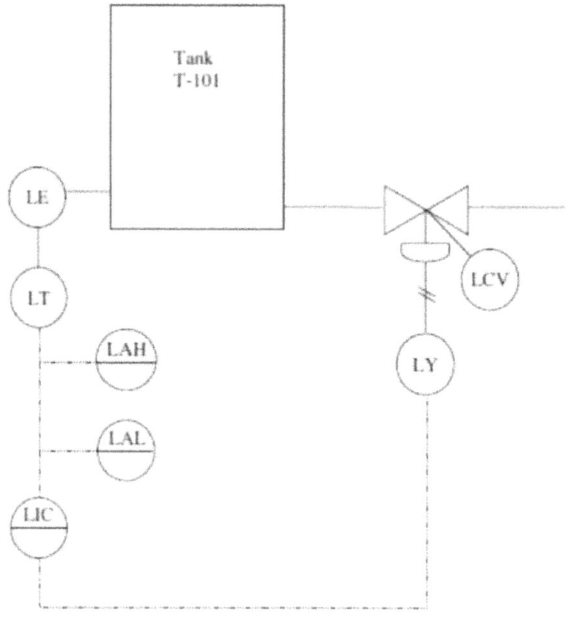

FIGURE 3.10: Example of a level control loop using P&ID symbols

TABLE 3.1: Common symbols used on P&IDs [Instrument Society of America Standard, ISA-5.1-1984 (R1992)]

Instrument Line Symbols

	Instrument supply or piping connection to process (capillary)
	Pneumatic
	Electrical
	Software signal

Instrument Location and Identification

(ABB)	Instrument located in plant
(ABB)	Instrument located on front of panel in control room
(ABB)	Instrument located on back of panel in control room
(ABB)	Instrument accessible as part of a distributed control system

Common Identification Letters Used in Instrument Symbols

Analysis	Alarm	Burner	Combustion
Conductivity	Flow rate	Voltage	Sensor element
Specific gravity	User choice	Glass	Viewing device
Current (electrical)	Hand	Indicate	Control station
Time or time schedule	Power	Level	Light or low
Moisture	Pressure	Orifice	Restriction
Middle or intermediate	Vacuum	Point	Quantity
Radioactivity or ratio	Record	Temperature	Switch
Viscosity or vibration	Transmit	Relay	Valve

Damper or louver	Control	Well	Event
Speed or frequency	Compute	Convert	Position Drive
Weight or force	High	Density	Humidity

3.10. Instrumentation error

3.10.1. Definition of error

The measurement error is defined as the difference between the true or actual value and the measured value. The true value is the average of the infinite number of measurements, and the measured value is the precise value.

3.10.2. Types of Errors in Measurement

The error may arise from the different source and are usually classified into the following types. These types are

1. Gross Errors
2. Systematic Errors
3. Random Errors

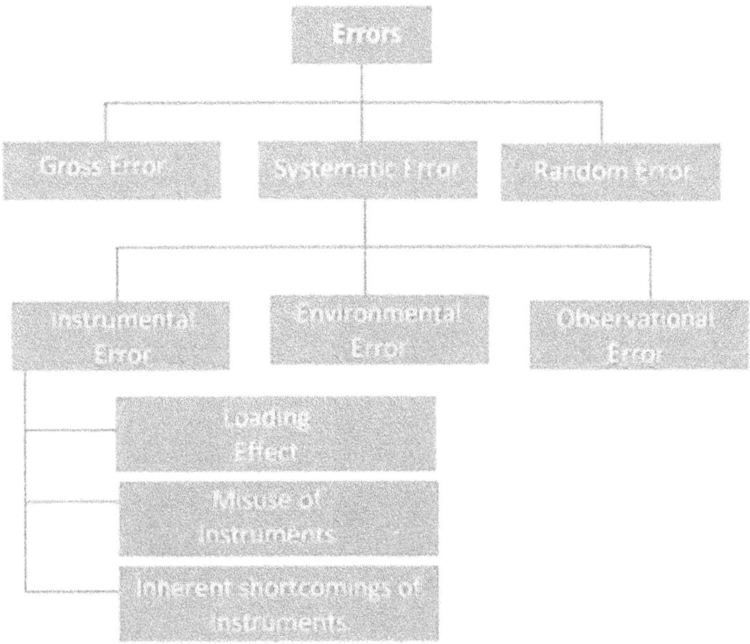

Their types are explained below in details:

1. Gross Errors

- The gross error occurs because of the human mistakes.

- For examples consider the person using the instruments takes the wrong reading, or they can record the incorrect data. Such type of error comes under the gross error.

- The gross error can only be avoided by taking the reading carefully.

- For example – The experimenter reads the 31.5°C reading while the actual reading is 21.5C°. This happens because of the oversights. The experimenter takes the wrong reading and because of which the error occurs in the measurement.

- Such type of error is very common in the measurement. The complete elimination of such type of error is not possible.

- Some of the gross error easily detected by the experimenter but some of them is difficult to find.

Two methods can remove the gross error. These methods are:

- The reading should be taken very carefully.

- Two or more readings should be taken of the measurement quantity. The readings are taken by the different experimenter and at a different point for removing the error.

2. Systematic Errors

The systematic errors are mainly classified into three categories.

1. Instrumental Errors

2. Environmental Errors

3. Observational Errors

2 (i) Instrumental Errors

These errors mainly arise due to the three main reasons.

(a) Inherent Shortcomings of Instruments – Such types of errors are inbuilt in instruments because of their mechanical structure. They may be due to manufacturing, calibration or operation of the device. These errors may cause the error to read too low or too high.

For example – If the instrument uses the weak spring then it gives the high value of measuring quantity. The error occurs in the instrument because of the friction or hysteresis loss.

(b) Misuse of Instrument – The error occurs in the instrument because of the fault of the operator. A good instrument used in an unintelligent way may give an enormous result.

For example – the misuse of the instrument may cause the failure to adjust the zero of instruments, poor initial adjustment, using lead to too high resistance. These improper practices may not cause permanent damage to the instrument, but all the same, they cause errors.

(c) Loading Effect – It is the most common type of error which is caused by the instrument in measurement work.

For example, when the voltmeter is connected to the high resistance circuit it gives a misleading reading, and when it is connected to the low resistance circuit, it gives the dependable reading. This means the voltmeter has a loading effect on the circuit.

The error caused by the loading effect can be overcome by using the meters intelligently. For example, when measuring a low resistance by the ammeter-voltmeter method, a voltmeter having a very high value of resistance should be used.

2 (ii) Environmental Errors

These errors are due to the external condition of the measuring devices. Such types of errors mainly occur due to the effect of temperature, pressure, humidity, dust, vibration or because of the magnetic or electrostatic field. The corrective measures employed to eliminate or to reduce these undesirable effects are

- The arrangement should be made to keep the conditions as constant as possible.
- Using the equipment which is free from these effects.
- By using the techniques which eliminate the effect of these disturbances.
- By applying the computed corrections.

2 (iii) Observational Errors

Such types of errors are due to the wrong observation of the reading. There are many sources of observational error.

For example, the pointer of a voltmeter resets slightly above the surface of the scale. Thus an error **occurs** (because of parallax) unless the line of vision of the observer is exactly above the pointer. To minimize the parallax error highly accurate meters are provided with mirrored scales.

3. Random Errors

The error which is caused by the sudden change in the atmospheric condition, such type of error is called random error. These types of error remain even after the removal of the systematic error. Hence such type of error is also called residual error.

3.11. Calibration of equipment

- Calibration of an instrument is the process of determining its accuracy.
- The process involves obtaining a reading from the instrument and measuring its variation from the reading obtained from a standard instrument.

- Calibration of an instrument also involves adjusting its precision and accuracy so that its readings come in accordance with the established standard.

3.11.1. What is Equipment Calibration?

Calibration of equipment needs to be carried out on a regular basis. This is because instruments tend to deviate owing to hard operating conditions, mechanical shocks or exposure to extreme temperature or pressure.

Frequency of calibration would depend on the tolerance level. When the objective of the measurement is critical calibration would need to be carried out more frequently and with great accuracy.

To assure accuracy in instrument calibration, it is vital to ensure that each component of the measuring instrument is conforming to its specified standard. Regular equipment calibration carried out in a set format helps you obtain valid data and operate in a safe working environment.

3.11.2. Types of Calibration

Instrument calibration can be carried out on different types of instruments across sectors. Discussed here are some of most frequently performed types of calibration services.

✓ **Pressure Calibration**

This is one of the most frequently performed types of equipment calibration. Under pressure calibration service gas and hydraulic pressure are typically measured across a variety of sectors. Various types of pressure balances and calibrators along with a number of pressure gages are used for carrying out pressure calibration.

Pressure instruments that are frequently calibrated include:

- Analogue Pressure Gauges
- Barometers
- Digital Indicators
- Digital Pressure Gauges
- Test Gauges
- Transmitters

✓ **Temperature Calibration**

Temperature calibration is carried out in all processes where temperature readings play a critical role. Temperature calibration is carried out in a controlled environment. State-of-the-art electrical and mechanical thermometers are available that can help in the process of temperature calibration. Temperature measuring equipment that requires calibration on a periodic basis includes:

- Chambers/Furnaces

- ➢ Data Acquisition Systems
- ➢ Dial Thermometers
- ➢ Infrared Meters
- ➢ PRTs and Thermistors
- ➢ Thermal Cameras
- ➢ Thermometers/Thermocouples
- ➢ Weather Stations
- ✓ **Flow Calibration**

Flow calibration services needs to be carried out on a routine basis for flow meters that check product or feedstock quality and quantity, fuel/energy quantity or function in a critical process.

The four main types of flow meters that frequently require calibration include:

- ➢ Laminar Flow meters
- ➢ Rotameter – Gas and Air
- ➢ Thermal Mass Flow meters
- ➢ Turbine Meters
- ✓ **Electrical calibration**

Electrical calibration is required for checking the veracity of electrical instruments across a diverse range of industries. Under electrical calibration elements such as current frequency, resistance and voltage are checked.

Instruments that are frequently sent for electrical calibration include:

- ➢ Clamp Meters
- ➢ Counter timers
- ➢ Data Loggers
- ➢ Electrical meters
- ➢ Insulation Testers
- ➢ Loop Testers
- ➢ Multi-meters
- ➢ Oscilloscopes
- ➢ RCD

- ✓ **Mechanical calibration**

Mechanical calibration services are invoked for a range of mechanical instruments. Under this process a number of elements such as mass, force, dimension, angle, volume, flatness, torque and vibration are calibrated in a temperature controlled facility. Some of the most frequently tested instruments for mechanical calibration include:

- ➢ Accelerometers
- ➢ Load Cells & Force Gauges
- ➢ Micrometres, Verniers, Height Gauges
- ➢ Scales/Balances
- ➢ Torque Wrenches & Screwdrivers

➢ Weight & Mass Sets

✓ **Process**

The exact process of equipment calibration shall vary according to the type of instrument, how critical its role is in the operation and standards that are followed for the calibration purpose. Mentioned below is a typical process that needs to be followed for equipment calibration.

➢ **Attention given to the instrument design:** When carrying out calibration, special attention should be given to the design of the instrument which is to be calibrated.

➢ **Follow instructions:** Instructions specified for carrying out equipment calibration should be followed closely. Deviation from instruction or use of wrong calibrator value may result in accuracy.

➢ **Check tolerance value:** Tolerance value of the instrument should be taken in regard. It may be noted that every calibrator has a particular tolerance level this is due to the normal variations in the instrumentation and quality control process.

The tolerance level will vary according to several factors including the industry sector and even the country in which the calibration process is to be carried out.

➢ **Accuracy ratio:** Maintaining accuracy ratio is also critical in a calibration process. This describes the accuracy of the test standard in comparison to the accuracy of the instrument which is to be calibrated. Ensuring at least 4:1 accuracy ratio is essential. This suggests that the accuracy of the standard should be at least four times greater that the instrument which is to be calculated.

➢ **Adhering to standards:** Adhering to internationally recognized standards is vital. Hence when calibrating equipment, all standard procedures established under nationally or internationally recognized standards need to be followed.

➢ **Make uncertainty analysis:** Uncertainty analysis is to be taken at the end of the calibration process. This helps to evaluate any factor that may have affected the results of calibration.

3.11.3. Need of Equipment Calibration

Calibration of equipment is not just desirable, it is rather a necessity. All measuring instruments, whether they are used in factories, laboratories or at home, need to be calibrated on a periodic basis to ensure they are offering accurate results.

However, in factories and laboratories, measurement results are usually of a critical value. Deviation from accuracy can not only affect productivity but also cause threat to the life of workers. Hence, it is imperative that instrument calibration be carried out carefully and at regular intervals.

3.12. Types of censors used in cement plant

When looking at the automation pyramid, it becomes obvious that instruments and sensors form the foundation for any control and automation. It is here where the information is gathered which is then used further in the automation pyramid for either:

- Interlocking and control for automated production
- Regulation with PID-controller and high level control to ease the workload of the operator and to improve the plant performance (reduce energy consumption and/or increase production)
- Display and register process values to inform the management and the operator about the plant performance

The task of an instrument or a sensor is to convert a physical value into an electrical signal. A signal is picked up with a primary element, then converted in the transmitter to an electrical signal and finally transmitted to a control centre where the signal is further treated for either display, alarming or control.

The example shows a pressure transmitter. The pressure (connected on either side) distorts the bellows. This deformation is moving a lever which is connected to a plunger moving in a coil. The movement of the plunger in the coil evokes an electrical signal which then is converted to a standard electrical signal of 4-20 mA.

All transmitters work on a physical principle which depends on the process media, the desired type of measurement and the accuracy required. Some principles are as simple as in the example given. Others, like gas analysers working on light diffraction are more sophisticated and therefore not only more expensive but as well prone to high maintenance.

Like in all engineering fields, instrumentation has its own kind of terminology; and to be able to read a technical specification these terms have to be known. The following list gives a short overview of the most important terms used.

Example Ampere meter .5% accuracy

Temperature meter $\pm$ 5o C

- Accuracy: A number of quantities (usually expressed in % full scale) which defines the maximum error.

- Calibration: The ascertain by the use of a standard the locations at which scale or chart graduation of an instrument should be placed to correspond to the required value. To adjust the output of an instrument to bring the desired value within a specified tolerance.

- Dead band: The range throughout which an input can be varied without initiating response. Dead band is usually expressed in percent of full span.

- Dead time: The interval of time between initiation of an input and the start of the resulting response.

- Damping: Reducing of the oscillation of a process input or the output of a controller.

- Drift: Undesired change of an output over a period of time.

- Deviation: Departure from a desired or expected value also difference between measured value and true value.

- Error: (see drift) Error = indication minus true value
  $$= \text{set point minus measured value}$$

- Elevated Zero: A range where the zero value is greater than the lower range value.

- Feedback: Positive answer to a demand in change

- Gain: Is the ratio of an output change to an input change. (Reciprocal to proportional band).

- Hysteresis: The maximum difference between the upscale and downscale indications of the measured signal during a full range traverse for the same input.

  (Alarm limits for example are equipped with a hysteresis in order to prevent repeated signals around the alarm point).

- Impedance: Resistance of a network of resistors, capacitors and/or inductors.

- Interference: Noise (spurious voltage or current arising from external sources or interference between measuring circuit and ground).

- Input: Device to convert the electrical signal into digital information for further treatment in a Process Station or Programmable Logic Controller (PLC).

- Linearity: The closeness to which a curve approximates a straight line.

- Limit: Alarm limit

- Lag: (Time lag) time elapsed between process and measuring point as well as measuring point and control device.

- Noise: False signal picked up in the transmission line (see interference and signal-to-noise ratio).

- Output: Signal from a device (instrument).

- Range: Region between limits of measuring device expressed by stating the lower and upper range values.

- Response: General behavior of the output of a device as a function of an input.

For additional information regarding PID control refer to the relevant paper in the process technology department.

- Sensitivity: (see dead band and gain).

- Signal to Noise Ratio: Ratio of signal amplitude to noise amplitude.

- Suppressed zero: The zero value of the measured variable is less than the lower range value. (Zero does not appear the scale).

- Time constant: Time required for an output of an instrument to complete 62.3% of the total rise or decay.

- Zero: Zero point of scale (to be calibrated frequently due to zero shifts resulting in parallel shift of the input output curve).

Chapter 4

Introduction to process measurement

4.1. Process measurement

Measurements are most commonly made in the SI system, which contains seven fundamental units: kilogram, meter, candela, second, ampere, kelvin, and mole.

Measurements are made or Measurements system is set up for one or more of the following functions:

1. To monitor processes and operations
2. To control processes and operations
3. To carry out same analysis

4.2. Static Characteristics of Instrument

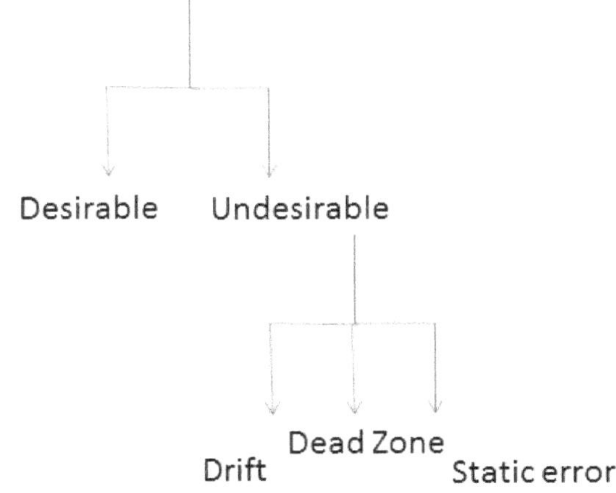

A device used to determine the present value of quantity under measurement.

Instrument may refer to:

1. Transducer
2. Signal conditioner and transmitter
3. Display/recording device

4.2.1. Accuracy

- The accuracy of an instrument is a measure of how close the output reading of the instrument is to the correct value.

- The accuracy of these two instruments depends on different things. For the first one it depends on the linearity and calibration of the spring, whilst for the second it relies on the calibration of the weights. As calibration of weights is much easier than careful choice and calibration of a linear-characteristic spring, this means that the second type of instrument will normally be the more accurate.

4.2.2. Precision

- Precision is a term that describes an instrument's degree of freedom from random errors.

- If a large number of readings are taken of the same quantity by a high precision instrument, then the spread of readings will be very small.

- Precision is often, though incorrectly, confused with accuracy. High precision does not imply anything about measurement accuracy. A high precision instrument may have a low accuracy. Low accuracy measurements from a high precision instrument are normally caused by a bias in the measurements, which is removable by recalibration.

4.2.3. Sensitivity

- The sensitivity of measurement is a measure of the change in instrument output that occurs when the quantity being measured changes by a given amount. Thus, sensitivity is the ratio:

$$\frac{\text{scale deflection}}{\text{value of measurand producing deflection}}$$

4.2.4. Repeatability

- The terms repeatability and reproducibility mean approximately the same but are applied in different contexts as given below.

- Repeatability describes the closeness of output readings when the same input is applied repetitively over a short period of time, with the same measurement conditions, same instrument and observer, same location and same conditions of use maintained throughout.

4.2.5. Reproducibility

- Reproducibility describes the closeness of output readings for the same input when there are changes in the method of measurement, observer, measuring instrument, location, conditions of use and time of measurement.

- Both terms thus describe the spread of output readings for the same input. This spread is referred to as repeatability if the measurement conditions are constant and as reproducibility if the measurement conditions vary.

4.2.6. Drift

- The actual change in the measurement value when the same characteristic is measured under the same conditions, same operator, at different points in time. Drift indicates how often a measurement needs recalibration.

- A dead band (sometimes called a neutral zone) is an interval of a signal domain or band where no action occurs (the system is dead). Dead band is used in voltage regulators and other controllers. The purpose is common; to prevent oscillation or repeated activation-deactivation cycles (called 'hunting' in proportional control systems).

4.2.7. Threshold

- If the input to an instrument is gradually increased from zero, the input will have to reach a certain minimum level before the change in the instrument output reading is of a large enough magnitude to be detectable. This minimum level of input is known as the *threshold* of the instrument.

- Creep describes the permanent deformation that an elastic element undergoes after it has been under load for a period of time. This can lead to significant measurement errors in the form of a bias on all readings if the instrument is not recalibrated from time to time. However, careful design and choice of materials can largely eliminate the problem.

4.2.8. Resolution

When an instrument is showing a particular output reading, there is a lower limit on the magnitude of the change in the input measured quantity that produces an observable change in the instrument output. Like threshold, *resolution* is sometimes specified as an absolute value and sometimes as a percentage of deflection. One of the major factors influencing the resolution of an instrument is how finely its output scale is divided into subdivisions.

The actual change in the measurement value when the same characteristic is measured under the same conditions, same operator, at different points in time. Drift indicates how often a measurement needs recalibration.

A dead band (sometimes called a neutral zone) is an interval of a signal domain or band where no action occurs (the system is dead). Dead band is used in voltage regulators and other controllers. The purpose is common; to prevent oscillation or repeated activation-deactivation cycles (called 'hunting' in proportional control systems).

The delay between the action and reaction of a measuring instrument; Hysteresis is the amount of error that results when this action occurs. Hysteresis is a non-linear effect. In this case the measuring instrument measures one set of values as its input is increased and another set of inconsistent values as the input is decreased.

Hysteresis is often due to the saturation of magnetic materials. Initially as the input level to the instrument is increased there is no saturation. At high level inputs the materials become saturated and change in behaviour. Then as the input level is reduced the instrument behaves differently because the measurements started from a saturated condition.

A creep-testing machine measures the Creep (the tendency of a material after being subjected to high levels of stress, e.g. high temperatures, to change its form in relation to time) of an object. It is a device that measures the alteration of a material after it has been put through different forms of stress.

Creep machines are important to see how much strain (load) an object can handle under pressure, so engineers and researchers are able to determine what materials to use. The device generates a creep time-dependent curve by calculating the steady rate of creep in reference to the time it takes for the material to change. Creep machines are primarily used by engineers to determine the stability of a material and its behavior when it is put through ordinary stresses.

4.3. Measurement resolution and accuracy

Resolution is the fineness to which an instrument can be read. The best measurement resolution that can be obtained with an ultrasonic ranging system is equal to the wavelength of the transmitted wave.

As wavelength is inversely proportional to frequency, high-frequency ultrasonic elements would seem to be preferable. There is a difference. Let's see it with an example. Here are two stopwatches. One is analogy and the other is digital. Both are manually actuated; this is an important point in the distinction.

First, let's look at the **resolution** of the two stopwatches: The analogy stopwatch has to be viewed on its dial. If you look closely, you can relate the big hand to the smallest tick-mark on the big dial. That tick mark is a tenth of a second. The best a good eye can do is resolving a reading to 1/10 second, which is therefore the **resolution** of the stopwatch.

The digital stopwatch has two digits beyond the seconds, so it subdivides time in hundredths of a second. Since it is easy to read to 1/100 of a second, that is its **resolution**. So there is a substantial difference between the watches in resolution-a power of ten, from 1/10 to 1/100 second.

4.4. Temperature measurement

Temperature is without doubt the most widely measured variable. Thermometers can be traced back to Galileo (1595). The importance of accurate temperature measurement cannot be overemphasized. In the process control of chemical reactions, temperature control is of major importance, since chemical reactions are temperature dependent.

All physical parameters are temperature-dependent, making it necessary in most cases to measure temperature along with the physical parameter, so that temperature corrections can be made to achieve accurate parameter measurements.

Instrumentation also can be temperature-dependent, requiring careful design or temperature correction, which can determine the choice of measurement device. For accurate temperature control, precise measurement of temperature is required.

4.5. Temperature Measuring Devices

The methods of measuring temperature can be categorized as follows:

1. Expansion of materials;

2. Electrical resistance change;

3. Thermistors;

4. Thermocouples;

5. Pyrometers;

6. Semiconductors.

4.5.1. Expansion of materials

Liquid in glass thermometers using mercury were, by far, the most common direct visual reading thermometer (if not the only one). Mercury also has the advantage of not wetting the glass; that is, the mercury cleanly traverses the glass tube without breaking into globules or coating the tube. The operating range of the mercury thermometer is from $-30°$ to $+800°F$ ($-35°$ to $+450°C$). The freezing point of mercury is $-38°F$ ($-38°C$).

The toxicity of mercury, ease of breakage, the introduction of cost-effective, accurate, and easily read digital thermometers, has brought about the demise of the mercury thermometer for room and clinical measurements. Other liquid in glass devices operate on the same principle as the mercury thermometer.

These other liquids have similar properties to mercury (e.g., have a high linear coefficient of expansion, are clearly visible, are non-wetting), but are nontoxic. The liquid in glass thermometers are used to replace the mercury thermometer, and to extend its operating range. These thermometers are inexpensive, and have good accuracy ($<0.1°C$) and linearity.

4.5.2. Electrical resistance change

RTDs are either a metal film deposited on a form or are wire-wound resistors, which are then sealed in a glass-ceramic composite material. Three-wire RTD encased in a stainless steel sheath for protection. The coil is wound to be non-inductive. The space between the element and the case is filled with a ceramic power for good thermal conduction. The element has three leads, so that correction can be made for voltage drops in the lead wires. The electrical resistance of pure metals is positive, increasing linearly with temperature.

4.5.3. Thermistors

Thermistors are a class of metal oxide (semiconductor material) that typically has a high negative temperature coefficient of resistance. They also can be positive. Thermistors have high sensitivity, which can be up to a 10% change per degree Celsius, making it the most sensitive temperature element available, but thermistors also have very nonlinear characteristics. The typical response time is from 0.5 to 5 seconds, with an operating range typically from $-50°$ to $+300°C$.

Devices are available with the temperature range extended to 500°C. Thermistors are low cost, and are manufactured in a wide range of shapes, sizes, and values.

When in use, care has to be taken to minimize the effects of internal heating. Thermistor materials have a temperature coefficient of resistance (α) given by:

$$\alpha = \frac{\Delta R}{R_s}\left(\frac{1}{\Delta T}\right)$$

(4.1)

Where, ΔR is the change in resistance due to a temperature change ΔT, and R_s is the material resistance at the reference temperature.

The nonlinear characteristics make the device difficult to use as an accurate measuring device without compensation, but its sensitivity and low cost makes it useful in many applications. The device is normally used in a bridge circuit, and padded with a resistor to reduce its nonlinearity.

4.5.4. Thermocouples

Thermocouples (T/C) are formed when two dissimilar metals are joined together to form a junction. Joining together the other ends of the dissimilar metals to form a second junction completes an electrical circuit. A current will flow in the circuit if the two junctions are at different temperatures.

The current flowing is the result of the difference in electromotive force developed at the two junctions due to their temperature difference. The voltage difference between the two junctions is measured, and this difference is proportional to the temperature difference between the two junctions.

Note that the thermocouple only can be used to measure temperature differences. However, if one junction is held at a reference temperature, then the voltage between the thermocouple junctions gives a measurement of the temperature of the second junction. An alternative method is to measure the temperature of the reference junction and apply a correction to the output signal. This method eliminates the need for constant temperature enclosures.

4.5.5. Pyrometers

Radiation can be used to sense temperature, by using devices called pyrometers, with thermocouples or thermopiles as the sensing element, or by using colour comparison devices. Pyrometers can be portable, and have a response time of a few milliseconds.

A thermopile is a number of thermocouples connected in series, which increases the sensitivity and accuracy by increasing the output voltage when measuring low temperature differences. Each of the reference junctions in the thermopile is returned to a common reference temperature.

Radiation pyrometers measure temperature by sensing the heat radiated from a hot body through a fixed lens, which focuses the heat energy on to a thermopile. This is a noncontact device. For instance, furnace temperatures are normally measured through a small hole in the furnace wall. The distance from the source to the pyrometer can be fixed, and the radiation should fill the field-of-view of the sensor.

The focusing lens and thermocouple setup using a thermopile as a detector. Optical pyrometers compare the incident radiation to the radiation from an internal filament. The current through the filament is adjusted until the radiation colours match. The current then can be directly related to the temperature of the radiation source. Optical pyrometers can be used to measure temperatures from 1,100° to 2,800°C, with an accuracy of ±.

4.5.6. Semiconductor Devices

Semiconductors have a number of parameters that vary linearly with temperature. Normally, the reference voltage of a zener diode or the junction voltage variations is used for temperature sensing. Semiconductor temperature sensors have a limited operating range, from −50° to +150°C, but are very linear, with accuracies of ±1°C or better.

Other advantages are that electronics can be integrated onto the same die as the sensor, giving high sensitivity, easy interfacing to control systems, and making possible different digital output configurations.

The thermal time constant varies from 1 to 5 seconds, and internal dissipation can cause up to a 0.5°C offset. Semiconductor devices also are rugged, have good longevity, and are inexpensive.

For the above reasons, the semiconductor sensor is used extensively in many applications, including the replacement of the mercury in glass thermometer.

4.6. Pressure Measurement

Pressure is the force exerted by gases and liquids due to their weight, such as the pressure of the atmosphere on the surface of the earth and the pressure containerized liquids exert on the bottom and walls of a container. Pressure units are a measure of the force acting over a specified area. It is most commonly expressed in pounds per square inch (psi), sometimes pounds per square foot (psf) in English units, or Pascal's (Pa or kPa) in metric units.

$$\text{Pressure} = \frac{\text{force}}{\text{area}}$$

(4.2)

4.6.1. Hydrostatic Pressure

The pressure at a specific depth in a liquid is termed hydrostatic pressure. The pressure increases as the depth in a liquid increases. This increase is due to the weight of the fluid above the measurement point. The pressure p is given by:

$$p = \gamma h$$

(4.3)

Where γ is the specific weight (lb/ft^3 in English units, or N/m^3 in SI units), and h is the distance from the surface in compatible units (e.g., ft, in, cm, or m).

4.6.2. Specific Gravity

The specific gravity (SG) of a liquid or solid is defined as the density of a material divided by the density of water. SG also can be defined as the specific weight of the material divided by the specific weight of water at a specified temperature.

The specific gravity of a gas is its density (or specific weight) divided by the density (or specific weight) of air at 60°F and 1 atmospheric pressure (14.7 psia). In the SI system, the density in grams per cubic centimeter or mega grams per cubic meter and the SG have the same value.

Both specific weight and density are temperature dependent parameters, so that the temperature should be specified when they are being measured. SG is a dimensionless value, since it is a ratio.

4.6.3. Units of Measurement

Many industrial processes operate at pressures that are referenced to atmospheric pressure, and are known as gauge pressures. Other processes operate at pressures referenced to a vacuum, or can be referred to as negative gauge pressure. Atmospheric pressure is not a fixed value, but depends on factors such as humidity, height above sea level, temperature, and so forth. The following terms exist when considering atmospheric constants.

1. Atmospheric pressure is measured in pounds per square inch (psi), in the English system.

2. Atmospheric pressure is measured in Pascal's (Pa or N/m^2), in the SI system.

3. Atmospheric pressure can be stated in inches or centimeters of water.

4. Atmospheric pressure can be stated in inches or millimeters of mercury.

5. Atmosphere (atm) is the equivalent pressure in atmospheres.

6. 1 torr = 1 mm mercury, in the metric system.

7. 1 bar (1.013 atm) = 100 kPa, in metric system.

There are six terms applied to pressure measurements. They are as follows:

Total vacuum–which is zero pressure or lack of pressure, as would be experienced in outer space.

Vacuum is a pressure measurement made between total vacuum and normal atmospheric pressure (14.7 psi).

Atmospheric pressure is the pressure on the earth's surface due to the weight of the gases in the earth's atmosphere and is normally expressed at sea level as 14.7 psi or 101.36 kPa. It is however, dependant on atmospheric conditions. The pressure decreases above sea level and at an elevation of 5000 ft drops to about 12.2 psi (84.122 kPa).

Absolute pressure is the pressure measured with respect to a vacuum and is expressed in pounds per square inch absolute (psia).

Gauge pressure is the pressure measured with respect to atmospheric pressure and is normally expressed in pounds per square inch gauge (psig). Figure 4.1 shows graphically the relation between atmospheric, gauge, and absolute pressures.

Differential pressure is the pressure measured with respect to another pressure and is expressed as the difference between the two values. This would represent two points in a pressure or flow system and is referred to as the delta p or Δp. Figure 4.2 shows two situations, where differential pressure exists across a barrier and between two points in a flow system.

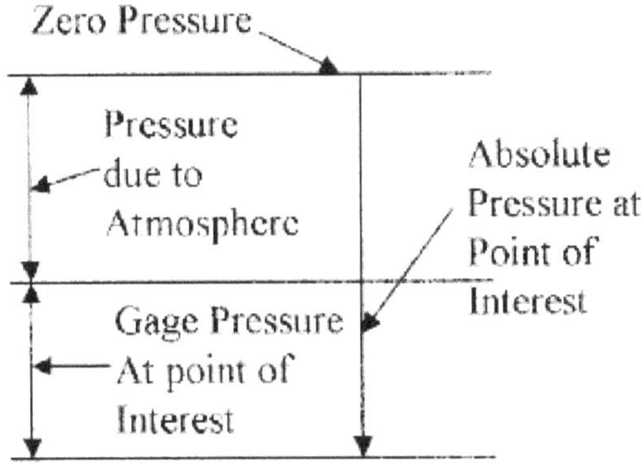

Figure: 4.1 Illustration of gauge pressure versus absolute pressure

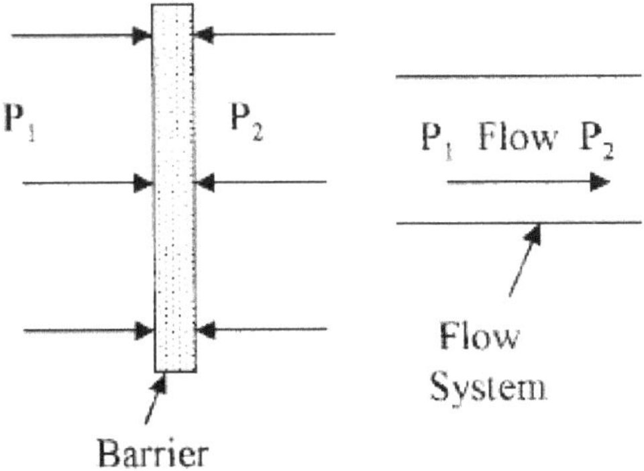

Figure 4.2: Illustration of delta or differential pressure

4.7. Liquid Level Measurement

The measurement of the liquid level and free flowing solids in containers, the detector is normally sensing the interface between a liquid and a gas, a solid and a gas, a solid and a liquid, or possibly the interface between two liquids.

Sensing liquid levels fall into two categories; firstly, single point sensing and secondly, continuous level monitoring. In the case of single point sensing the actual level of the material is detected when it reaches a predetermined level, so that the appropriate action can be taken to prevent overflowing or to refill the container.

Continuous level monitoring measures the level of the liquid on an uninterrupted basis. In this case the level of the material will be constantly monitored and hence, the volume can be calculated if the cross-sectional area of the container is known.

Level measurements can be direct or indirect; examples of these are using a float technique or measuring pressure and calculating the liquid level. Free flowing solids are dry powders, crystals, rice, grain and so forth.

4.7.1. Level Formulas

Pressure is often used as an indirect method of measuring liquid levels. Pressure increases as the depth increases in a fluid. The pressure is given by

$$\Delta p = \gamma \Delta h \tag{4.4}$$

Where Δp = change in pressure

γ = specific weight

Δh = depth

Note the units must be consistent, i.e., pounds and feet, or newton's and meters. Buoyancy is an indirect method used to measure liquid levels.

The level is determined using the buoyancy of an object partially immersed in a liquid. The buoyancy B or upward force on a body in a liquid can be calculated from the equation

$$B = \gamma \times \text{area} \times d \tag{4.5}$$

Where area is the cross-sectional area of the object and d is the immersed depth of the object.

The liquid level is then calculated from the weight of a body in a liquid W_L, which is equal to its weight in air (W_A – B), from which we get

$$d = \frac{W_A - W_L}{\gamma \times \text{area}} \tag{4.6}$$

The weight of a container can be used to calculate the level of the material in the container. In Figure 4.3 the volume V of the material in the container is given by

$$V = \text{area} \times \text{depth} = \pi r^2 \times d$$

(4.7)

Where r is the radius of the container and d is the depth of the material.

The weight of material W in a container is given by capacitive probes can be used in nonconductive liquids and free flowing solids for level measurement.

$$W = \gamma V$$

(4.8)

Many materials, when placed between the plates of a capacitor, increase the capacitance by a factor m called the dielectric constant of the material. For instance, air has a dielectric constant of 1 and water 80.

Figure 4.4 shows two capacitor plates partially immersed in a nonconductive liquid. The capacitance (Cd) is given by

$$Cd = Ca\mu\frac{d}{r} + Ca$$

(4.9)

Where C_α = capacitance with no liquid

m = dielectric constant of the liquid between the plates

r = height of the plates

d = depth or level of the liquid between the plates

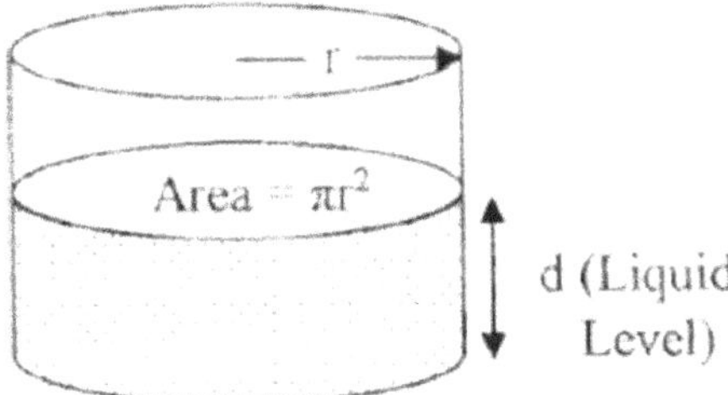

Figure 4.3 Shows the relation between volume of liquid and the cross- sectional area and the liquid depth

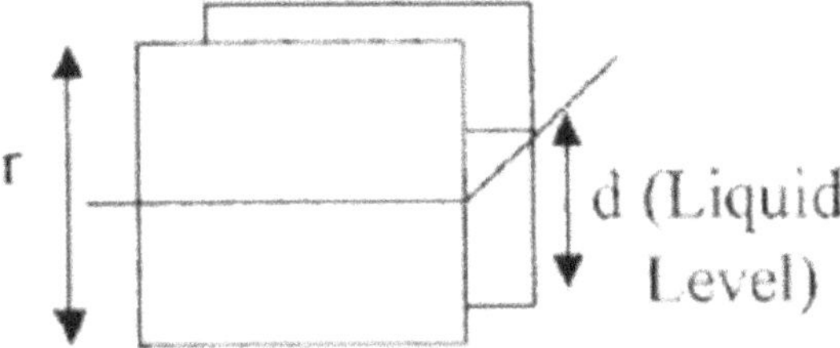

Figure 4.4 Shows the relation between liquid level, plate capacitance, and a known dielectric constant in a non-conducting liquid

The dielectric constants of some common liquids are large variations in dielectric constant with temperature so that temperature correction may be needed. In above equation the liquid level is given by

$$d = \frac{(Cd - Ca)}{\mu Ca} r$$

(4.10)

4.7.2. Level Sensing Devices

There are two categories of level sensing devices. They are direct sensing, in which case the actual level is monitored, and indirect sensing where a property of the liquid such as pressure is sensed to determine the liquid level.

4.8. Flow level measurement (gas & liquid)

Velocity is a measure of speed and direction of an object. When related to fluids it is the rate of flow of fluid particles in a pipe. The speed of particles in a fluid flow varies across the flow, i.e., where the fluid is in contact with the constraining walls (the boundary layer) the velocity of the liquid particles is virtually zero; in the center of the flow the liquid particles will have the maximum

Velocity: Thus, the average rate of flow is used in flow calculations. The units of flow are normally feet per second (fps), feet per minute (fpm), meters per second (mps), and so on. Previously, the pressures associated with fluid flow were defined as static, impact, or dynamic.

Laminar flow of a liquid occurs when its average velocity is comparatively low and the fluid particles tend to move smoothly in layers, as shown in Figure 4.5. The velocity of the particles across the liquid takes a parabolic shape.

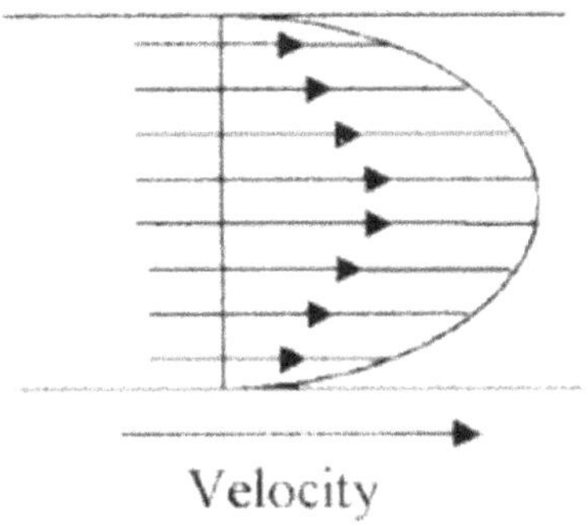

Figure 4.5: Flow velocity variations across a pipe with laminar flow

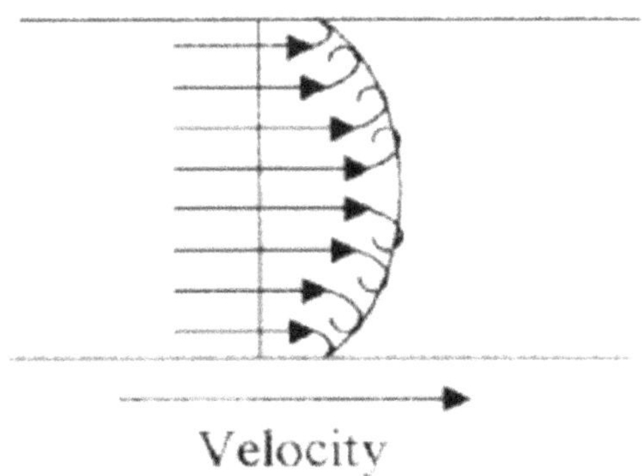

Figure 4.6: Flow velocity variations across a pipe with turbulent flow

Turbulent flow occurs when the flow velocity is high and the particles no longer flow smoothly in layers and turbulence or a rolling effect occurs. This is shown in Figure 4.6. Note also the flattening of the velocity profile.

Viscosity is a property of a gas or liquid that is a measure of its resistance to motion or flow. A viscous liquid such as syrup has a much higher viscosity than water and water has a higher viscosity than air. Syrup, because of its high viscosity, flows very slowly and it is very hard to move an object through it. Viscosity (dynamic) can be measured in poise or centipoise, whereas kinematic viscosity (without force) is measured in stokes or centistokes. Dynamic or absolute viscosity is used in the Reynolds and flow equations. Typically the viscosity of a liquid decreases as temperature increases.

The Reynolds number R is a derived relationship combining the density and viscosity of a liquid with its velocity of flow and the cross-sectional dimensions of the flow and takes the form

$$R = \frac{VD\rho}{\mu}$$

(4.11)

Where V = average fluid velocity

D = diameter of the pipe

ρ = density of the liquid

μ = absolute viscosity

Flow patterns can be considered to be laminar, turbulent, or a combination of both. Osborne Reynolds observed in 1880 that the flow pattern could be predicted from physical properties of the liquid.

If the Reynolds number for the flow in a pipe is equal to or less than 2000 the flow will be laminar. From 2000 to about 5000 is the intermediate region where the flow can be laminar, turbulent, or a mixture of both, depending upon other factors. Beyond 5000 the flow is always turbulent.

The Bernoulli equation is an equation for flow based on the law of conservation of energy, which states that the total energy of a fluid or gas at any one point in a flow is equal to the total energy at all other points in the flow.

Energy factors: Most flow equations are based on the law of energy conservation and relate the average fluid or gas velocity, pressure, and the height of fluid above a given reference point. This relationship is given by the Bernoulli equation. The equation can be modified to take into account energy losses due to friction and increase in energy as supplied by pumps.

Energy losses in flowing fluids are caused by friction between the fluid and the containment walls and by fluid impacting an object. In most cases these losses should be taken into account. Whilst these equations apply to both liquids and gases, they are more complicated in gases because of the fact that gases are compressible.

Flow rate is the volume of fluid passing a given point in a given amount of time and is typically measured in gallons per minute (gpm), cubic feet per minute (cfm), liter per minute, and so on.

Total flow is the volume of liquid flowing over a period of time and is measured in gallons, cubic feet, liters and so forth.

4.9. Flow Formulas for flow level measurement

4.9.1. Continuity equation

The continuity equation states that if the overall flow rate in a system is not changing with time, the flow rate in any part of the system is constant.

From which we get the following equation:

$$Q = VA \qquad (4.12)$$

Where Q = flow rate

V = average velocity

A = cross-sectional area of the pipe

The units on both sides of the equation must be compatible, i.e., English units or metric units.

4.9.2. Bernoulli equation

The Bernoulli equation gives the relation between pressure, fluid velocity, and elevation in a flow system. The equation is accredited to Bernoulli (1738). When applied the following is obtained-

$$\frac{P_A}{\gamma_A} + \frac{V_A^2}{2g} + Z_A = \frac{P_B}{\gamma_B} + \frac{V_B^2}{2g} + Z_B$$

(4.13)

Where P_A and P_B = absolute static pressures at points A and B, respectively

γ_A and γ_B = specific weights

V_A and V_B = average fluid velocities

g = acceleration of gravity

Z_A and Z_B = elevations above a given reference level, i.e., $Z_A - Z_B$ is the head of fluid.

The units in Bernoulli equation are consistent and reduce to units of length (feet in the English system and meter in the SI system of units) as follows:

$$\text{Pressure energy} = \frac{p}{\gamma} = \frac{\text{lb/ft}^2(\text{N/m}^2)}{\text{lb/ft}^3(\text{N/m}^3)} = \text{ft(m)}$$

(4.14)

$$\text{Kinetic energy} = \frac{V^2}{g} = \frac{(\text{ft/s})^2(\text{m/s})^2}{\text{ft/s}^2(\text{m/s}^2)} = \text{ft(m)}$$

(4.15)

$$\text{Potential energy} = Z = \text{ft(m)}$$

(4.16)

4.9.3. Flow losses

The Bernoulli equation does not take into account flow losses; these losses are accounted for by pressure losses and fall into two categories. Firstly, those associated with viscosity and the friction between the constriction walls and the flowing fluid, and secondly, those associated with fittings, such as valves, elbows, tees, and so forth.

Outlet losses: The flow rate Q from the continuity equation for instance gives

$$Q = V_3 A_3 \tag{4.17}$$

However, to account for losses at the outlet, the equation should be modified to

$$Q = C_D V_3 A_3 \tag{4.18}$$

Where, C_D is the discharge coefficient that is dependent on the shape and size of the orifice. The discharge coefficients can be found in flow data.

Frictional losses: They are losses from liquid flow in a pipe due to friction between the flowing liquid and the restraining walls of the container. These frictional losses are given by

$$h_L = \frac{fLV^2}{2\,Dg} \tag{4.19}$$

Where h_L = head loss

f = friction factor

L = length of pipe

D = diameter of pipe

V = average fluid velocity

g = gravitation constant

The friction factor f depends on the Reynolds number for the flow and the roughness of the pipe walls.

4.10. Weight measurement

- In science and engineering, the weight of an object is the force acting on the object due to gravity.

- Weight defined as a vector quantity, the gravitational force acting on the object. Others define weight as a scalar quantity, the magnitude of the gravitational force.

- Yet others define it as the magnitude of the reaction force exerted on a body by mechanisms that counteract the effects of gravity: the weight is the quantity that is measured by, for example, a spring scale.

- Thus, in a state of free fall, the weight would be zero. In this sense of weight, terrestrial objects can be weightless: ignoring air resistance, the famous apple falling from the tree, on its way to meet the ground near Isaac Newton, would be weightless.

- The unit of measurement for weight is that of force, which in the International System (SI), Unit is the newton. For example, an object with a mass of one kilogram has a weight of about 9.8 newtons on the surface of the Earth, and about one-sixth as much on the Moon.

- Although weight and mass are scientifically distinct quantities, the terms are often confused with each other in everyday use (i.e. comparing and converting force weight in pounds to mass in kilograms and vice versa).

Further complications in elucidating the various concepts of weight have to do with the theory of relativity according to which gravity is modeled as a consequence of the curvature of space-time. In the teaching community, a considerable debate has existed for over half a century on how to define weight for their students. The current situation is that a multiple set of concepts co-exist and find use in their various contexts.

4.11. Newton

- The introduction of Newton's laws of motion and the development of Newton's law of universal gravitation led to considerable further development of the concept of weight.

- Weight became fundamentally separate from mass. Mass was identified as a fundamental property of objects connected to their inertia, while weight became identified with the force of gravity on an object and therefore dependent on the context of the object. In particular, Newton considered weight to be relative to another object causing the gravitational pull, e.g. the weight of the Earth towards the Sun.

- Newton considered time and space to be absolute. This allowed him to consider concepts as true position and true velocity. Newton also recognized that weight as measured by the action of weighing was affected by environmental factors such as buoyancy. He considered this a false weight induced by imperfect measurement conditions, for which he introduced the term *apparent weight* as compared to the *true weight* defined by gravity.

- Although Newtonian physics made a clear distinction between weight and mass, the term weight continued to be commonly used when people meant mass. This led the 3rd General Conference on Weights and Measures (CGPM) of 1901 to officially declare "The word *weight* denotes a quantity of the same nature as a *force*: the weight of a body is the product of its mass and the acceleration due to gravity", thus distinguishing it from mass for official usage.

Definition

In the ISO International standard ISO 80000-4:2006, describing the basic physical quantities and units in mechanics as a part of the International standard ISO/IEC 80000, the definition of *weight* is given as:

$$F_g = mg \tag{4.20}$$

Where, m is mass and g is local acceleration of free fall.

Remarks

- When the reference frame is Earth, this quantity comprises not only the local gravitational force, but also the local centrifugal force due to the rotation of the Earth, a force which varies with latitude.

- The effect of atmospheric buoyancy is excluded in the weight.

- In common parlance, the name "weight" continues to be used where "mass" is meant, but this practice is deprecated.

The definition is dependent on the chosen frame of reference. When the chosen frame is co-moving with the object in question then this definition precisely agrees with the operational definition. If the specified frame is the surface of the Earth, the weight according to the ISO and gravitational definitions differ only by the centrifugal effects due to the rotation of the Earth.

4.12. Mass

In modern scientific usage, weight and mass are fundamentally different quantities: mass is an intrinsic property of matter, whereas weight is a *force* that results from the action of gravity on matter: it measures how strongly the force of gravity pulls on that matter. However, in most practical everyday situations the word "weight" is used when, strictly, "mass" is meant. For example, most people would say that an object "weighs one kilogram", even though the kilogram is a unit of mass.

The distinction between mass and weight is unimportant for many practical purposes because the strength of gravity does not vary too much on the surface of the Earth. In a uniform gravitational field, the gravitational force exerted on an object (its weight) is directly proportional to its mass.

For example, object a weighs 10 times as much as object B, so therefore the mass of object A is 10 times greater than that of object B. This means that an object's mass can be measured indirectly by its weight, and so, for everyday purposes, weighing (using a weighing scale) is an entirely acceptable way of measuring mass. Similarly, a balance measures mass indirectly by comparing the weight of the measured item to that of an object(s) of known mass. Since the measured item and the comparison mass are in virtually the same location, so experiencing the same gravitational field, the effect of varying gravity does not affect the comparison or the resulting measurement.

The Earth's gravitational field is not uniform but can vary by as much as 0.5% at different locations on Earth (see Earth's gravity). These variations alter the relationship between weight and mass, and must be taken into account in high-precision weight measurements that are intended to indirectly measure mass. Spring scales, which measure local weight, must be calibrated at the location at which the objects will be used to show this standard weight, to be legal for commerce.

The historical use of "weight" for "mass" also persists in some scientific terminology – for example, the chemical terms "atomic weight", "molecular weight", and "formula weight", can still be found rather than the preferred "atomic mass", etc.

In a different gravitational field, for example, on the surface of the Moon, an object can have a significantly different weight than on Earth. The gravity on the surface of the Moon is only about one-sixth as strong as on the surface of the Earth. A one-kilogram mass is still a one-kilogram mass (as mass is an intrinsic property of the object) but the downward force due to gravity, and therefore its weight, is only one-sixth of what the object would have on Earth. So a man of mass 180 pounds weighs only about 30 pounds-force when visiting the Moon.

SI units

In most modern scientific work, physical quantities are measured in SI units. The SI unit of weight is the same as that of force: the newton (N) – a derived unit which can also be expressed in SI base units as $kg \cdot m/s^2$ (kilograms times metres per second squared).

In commercial and everyday use, the term "weight" is usually used to mean mass, and the verb "to weigh" means "to determine the mass of" or "to have a mass of". Used in this sense, the proper SI unit is the kilogram (kg).

Pound and other non-SI units

In United States customary units, the pound can be either a unit of force or a unit of mass. Related units used in some distinct, separate subsystems of units include the poundal and the slug. The poundal is defined as the force necessary to accelerate an object of one-pound *mass* at 1 ft/s^2, and is equivalent to about 1/32.2 of a pound-*force*. The slug is defined as the amount of mass that accelerates at 1 ft/s^2 when one pound-force is exerted on it, and is equivalent to about 32.2 pounds (mass).

The kilogram-force is a non-SI unit of force, defined as the force exerted by a one-kilogram mass in standard Earth gravity (equal to 9.80665 newtons exactly). The dyne is the cgs unit of force and is not a part of SI, while weights measured in the CGS unit of mass, the gram, remain a part of SI.

4.13. Measuring of mass

Weight is commonly measured using one of two methods. A spring scale or hydraulic or pneumatic scale measures local weight, the local force of gravity on the object (strictly *apparent* weight force). Since the local force of gravity can vary by up to 0.5% at different locations, spring scales will measure slightly different weights for the same object (the same mass) at different locations.

To standardize weights, scales are always calibrated to read the weight an object would have at a nominal standard gravity of 9.80665 m/s^2. However, this calibration is done at the factory. When the scale is moved to another location on Earth, the force of gravity will be different, causing a slight error. So to be highly accurate and legal for commerce, spring scales must be re-calibrated at the location at which they will be used.

A *balance* on the other hand, compares the weight of an unknown object in one scale pan to the weight of standard masses in the other, using a lever mechanism – a lever-balance. The standard masses are often referred to, non-technically, as "weights". Since any variations in gravity will act equally on the unknown and the known weights, a lever-balance will indicate the same value at any location on Earth.

Therefore, balance "weights" are usually calibrated and marked in mass units, so the lever-balance measures mass by comparing the Earth's attraction on the unknown object and standard masses in the scale pans. In the absence of a gravitational field, away from planetary bodies (e.g. space), a lever-balance would not work, but on the Moon, for example, it would give the same reading as on Earth. Some balances are marked in weight units, but since the weights are calibrated at the factory for standard gravity, the balance will measure standard weight, i.e. what the object would weigh at standard gravity, not the actual local force of gravity on the object.

If the actual force of gravity on the object is needed, this can be calculated by multiplying the mass measured by the balance by the acceleration due to gravity – either standard gravity (for everyday work) or the precise local gravity (for precision work).

Gross weight is a term that is generally found in commerce or trade applications, and refers to the total weight of a product and its packaging. Conversely, net weight refers to the weight of the product alone, discounting the weight of its container or packaging; and tare weight is the weight of the packaging alone.

4.14. Electrical energy and power measurement

Electrical power can be in the form of either direct current (dc) (one direction only) or alternating current (ac) (the current reverses periodically, see Figure 4.7). In ac circuits the electromotive force drives the current in one direction then reverses itself and drives the current in the reverse direction. The rate of direction change is expressed as a frequency f and is measured in hertz (Hz), i.e., cycles per second.

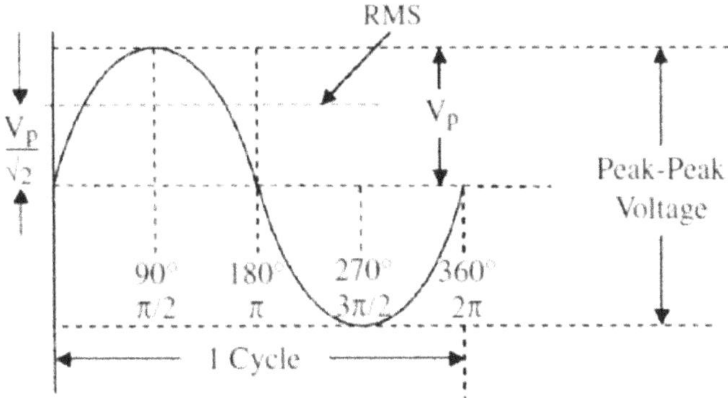

Figure 4.7 The basic sine wave

Electrical signals travel at the speed of light. The distance traversed in one cycle is called a wavelength *l*, the relationship between frequency and wavelength (meters) is given by the following equation:

$$f = \frac{c}{\lambda}$$

(4.21)

Where, *c* is the speed of light (3×108 m/s).

4.14.1. Resistance measurement

It is assumed that the student is familiar with the terms insulators, conductors, semiconductors, electrical resistance, capacitance, and inductance. Hence, the basic equations commonly used in electricity will be considered as a starting point.

The resistivity *r* of a material is the resistance to current flow between the opposite faces of a unit cube of

153

the material (ohm per unit length). The resistance R of a component is expressed by

$$R = \frac{\rho l}{A}$$

(4.22)

where l is the length of the material (distance between contacts), and A is the cross-sectional area of the resistor; l and A must be in compatible units.

Ohm's law applies to both dc and ac circuits, and states that in an electrical circuit the electromotive force (emf) will cause a current I to flow in a resistance R, such that the emf is equal to the current times the resistance, i.e.

$$E = IR$$

(4.23)

This can also be written as

$$I = E/R$$

(4.24)

Or

$$R = E/I$$

(4.25)

where E = electromotive force in volts (V)

I = current in amperes (A)

R = resistance in ohms (Ω)

Power transmission is more efficient over high-voltage lines at low current than at lower voltages and higher currents.

4.14.2. Resistor combinations

Resistors can be connected in series, parallel, or a combination of both in a resistor network. Resistors in series are connected, their effective total value RT is the sum of the individual resistors, and is given by

$$R_T = R_1 + R_2 + R_3 + \cdots + R_n$$

$$(4.26)$$

Resistors in parallel are connected, and their total effective value RT is given by

$$\frac{1}{R_T} = \frac{1}{R_1} + \frac{1}{R_2} + \frac{1}{R_3} + \cdots + \frac{1}{R_n}$$

$$(4.27)$$

Kirchhoff's laws apply to both dc and ac circuits. The first law (voltage law) states that in any closed path in a circuit, the algebraic sum of the voltages is zero, or the sum of the voltage drops across each component in a series circuit is equal to the source voltage. We get:

$$-E + V_1 + V_2 + V_3 = 0$$

$$(4.28)$$

Or

$$E = V_1 + V_2 + V_3$$

$$(4.29)$$

Kirchhoff's second law (current law) state that the sum of the currents at any node or junction is zero, i.e., the current flowing into a node is equal to the current flowing out of the node. In the upper node we get:

$$-I_T + I_1 + I_2 + I_3 = 0$$
(4.30)

Or

$$I_T = I_1 + I_2 + I_3$$
(4.31)

4.14.3. Capacitor formulas

Capacitors store electrical charge, as opposed to cells where the charge is generated by chemical action. Capacitance is a measure of the amount of charge that can be stored. The capacitance of a capacitor is given by

$$C = eA/d$$
(4.32)

Where, C = capacitance in farads (F)

e = dielectric constant of the material (F/m) between the plates

A = area of the plates (m2)

d = distance between the plates (m)

4.14.4. Capacitor combinations

The formulas for the effective capacitance of capacitors connected in series and parallel are the opposite of resistors connected in series and parallel. Capacitors in series and have an effective capacitance given by

$$\frac{1}{C_T} = \frac{1}{C_1} + \frac{1}{C_2} + \frac{1}{C_3} + \cdots + \frac{1}{C_n}$$

$$(4.33)$$

Capacitors in parallel and have an effective capacitance given by

$$C_T = C_1 + C_2 + C_3 + \cdots + C_n$$

$$(4.34)$$

4.14.5. Inductor formulas

Inductors are devices that oppose any change in the current flowing through them. The inductance of a coil is given by

$$L = \frac{N^2 \mu A}{d}$$

$$(4.35)$$

Where, L = inductance in henries

N = number of turns of wire

m = permeability of the core of the coil (H/m)

A = cross sectional area of the coil (m2)

d = length of the coil (m)

A henry is defined as the inductance that will produce an emf of 1 V when the current through the inductance changes at the rate of 1 A/s.

4.14.6. Inductor combinations

The formula for the effective inductance of inductors connected in series and parallel is the same as for resistors.

Inductors in series have an effective inductance given by

$$L_T = L_1 + L_2 + L_3 + \cdots + L_n$$

$$(4.36)$$

Inductors in parallel have an effective inductance given by

$$\frac{1}{L_T} = \frac{1}{L_1} + \frac{1}{L_2} + \frac{1}{L_3} + \cdots + \frac{1}{L_n}$$

$$(4.37)$$

- Introduction to the different effects of dc and ac electrical supplies on circuit components.

- Resistivity of materials and their resistance when made into components, the effect of temperature on the resistance of components, introduction to Ohm's law, and power dissipation in resistive components.

- The effective resistance of resistors connected in series and parallel and their use as voltage dividers.

- Discussion of Kirchhoff's voltage and current laws, Wheatstone bridge circuits and their use in the measurement of small changes in resistance, and the use of bridge circuits for strain gauge measurement.

- Description of capacitance and the formulas used for capacitors, the effective capacitance of capacitors connected in series and parallel and the impedance of capacitors when used in ac circuits.

> A description of inductance and the formulas used for inductors, the effective impedance of inductors used in ac circuits, and the effective inductance of inductors when they are connected in series and parallel.

4.15. Analytical measurement

- In the ordinary sense the term "analytical procedure" means a description of what has to be done while performing an analysis without reference to quality of the measurement.

- A more sound definition of "analytical procedure" can be given in terms of measurement (quality) assurance, in which a specified procedure to be followed is explicitly associated with an established accuracy of the results produced.

- The logic and consequences of such an approach are discussed, with background definitions and terminology as a starting point. Close attention is paid to the concept of measurement uncertainty as providing a single-number index of accuracy inherent in the procedure.

- The appropriateness of the uncertainty-based approach to analytical measurement is stressed in view of specific inaccuracy sources such as sampling and matrix effects. And methods for their evaluation are outlined. The question of a clear criterion for analytical procedure validation is also addressed from the standpoint of the quality requirement which measurement results need to meet as an end-product.

- **Analytical chemistry** studies and uses instruments and methods used to separate, identify, and quantify matter. In practice, separation, identification or quantification may constitute the entire analysis or be combined with another method. Separation isolates analyses.

- Qualitative analysis identifies analyses, while quantitative analysis determines the numerical amount or concentration.

- Analytical chemistry consists of classical, wet chemical methods and modern, instrumental methods.

- Classical qualitative methods use separations such as precipitation, extraction, and distillation. Identification may be based on differences in colour, odour, melting point, boiling point, radioactivity or reactivity.

- Classical quantitative analysis uses mass or volume changes to quantify amount. Instrumental methods may be used to separate samples using chromatography, electrophoresis or field flow fractionation.

- Then qualitative and quantitative analysis can be performed, often with the same instrument and may use light interaction, heat interaction, electric fields or magnetic fields. Often the same instrument can separate, identify and quantify analyse.

- Analytical chemistry is also focused on improvements in experimental design, chemo metrics, and the creation of new measurement tools. Analytical chemistry has broad applications to medicine, science and engineering.

4.16. Principles of analytical measurement

The results of analytical measurements need to be fit for their purpose and results obtained in different locations or at different times should be consistent. Laboratories make measurements to fulfill specific customer requirements.

If results are not fit for purpose then performing the analysis is a waste of time and money. If a laboratory knows, or suspects, that results are unreliable then it will incur the costs associated with repeating the measurements. The release of unreliable results to customers carries a risk and therefore a potentially significant cost to the laboratory.

Valid measurements and agreement between laboratories can be achieved by implementing a set of basic principles. The six principles of Valid Analytical Measurement provide a framework to enable organizations to deliver reliable results first time, every time, and achieve bottom line improvements through increased operational efficiency and reduction in risk. Laboratories that adopt valid analytical measurement provide customers and users of data with increased confidence that results of analytical measurements are valid and fit for purpose.

The valid analytical measurement Principles were developed as part of the Valid Analytical Measurement Programme, to set out a philosophy which is appropriate for any laboratory carrying out analytical measurements. The principles were designed to encapsulate the key issues for achieving valid measurements and to provide a useful reminder for those already familiar with the concepts.

Principle 1 Analytical measurements should be made to satisfy an agreed requirement.

Principle 2 Analytical measurements should be made using methods and equipment which have been tested to ensure they are fit for purpose

Principle 3 Staff making analytical measurements should be both qualified and competent to undertake the task.

Principle 4 There should be a regular independent assessment of the technical performance of a laboratory.

Principle 5 Analytical measurements made in one location should be consistent with that elsewhere.

Principle 6 Organizations making analytical measurements should have well defined quality control and quality assurance procedures.

4.17. Process Information Measurement

- Measurement is fundamental to the sciences; to engineering, construction, and other technical fields; and to almost all everyday activities.

- For that reason the elements, conditions, limitations, and theoretical foundations of measurement have been much studied. See also measurement system for a comparison of different systems and the history of their development.

- Measurements may be made by unaided human senses, in which case they are often called estimates, or, more commonly, by the use of instruments, which may range in complexity from simple rules for measuring lengths to highly sophisticated systems designed to detect and measure quantities entirely beyond the capabilities of the senses, such as radio waves from a distant star or the magnetic moment of a subatomic particle.

- Measurement begins with a definition of the quantity that is to be measured, and it always involves a comparison with some known quantity of the same kind.

- If the object or quantity to be measured is not accessible for direct comparison, it is converted or "transduced" into an analogous measurement signal.

- Since measurement always involves some interaction between the object and the observer or observing instrument, there is always an exchange of energy, which, although in everyday applications is negligible, can become considerable in some types of measurement and thereby limit accuracy.

- Measurement theory is the study of how numbers are assigned to objects and phenomena, and its concerns include the kinds of things that can be measured, how different measures relate to each other, and the problem of error in the measurement process. Any general theory of measurement must come to grips with three basic problems: error; representation, which is the justification of number assignment; and uniqueness, which is the degree to which the kind of representation chosen approaches being the only one possible for the object or phenomenon.

4.18. Measurement instruments and systems

- In general, measuring systems comprise a number of functional elements. One element is required to discriminate the object and sense its dimensions or frequency. This information is then transmitted throughout the system by physical signals.

- If the object is itself active, such as water flow, it may power the signal; if passive, it must trigger the signal by interaction either with an energetic probe, such as a light source or X-ray tube, or with a carrier signal.

- Eventually the physical signal is compared with a reference signal of known quantity that has been subdivided or multiplied to suit the range of measurement required. The reference signal is derived from objects of known quantity by a process called calibration.

- The comparison may be an analog process in which signals in a continuous dimension are brought to equality. An alternative comparison process is quantization by counting, i.e., dividing the signal into parts of equal and known size and adding up the number of parts.

- Other functions of measurement systems facilitate the basic process described above. Amplification ensures that the physical signal is strong enough to complete the measurement.

- In order to reduce degradation of the measurement as it progresses through the system, the signal may be converted to coded or digital form. Magnification, enlarging the measurement signal without increasing its power, is often necessary to match the output of one element of the system with the input of another, such as matching the size of the readout meter with the discerning power of the human eye.

- One important type of measurement is the analysis of resonance, or the frequency of variation within a physical system. This is determined by harmonic analysis, commonly exhibited in the sorting of signals by a radio receiver. Computation is another important measurement process, in which measurement signals are manipulated mathematically, typically by some form of analog or digital computer.

- Computers may also provide a control function in monitoring system performance.

- Measuring systems may also include devices for transmitting signals over great distances.

- All measuring systems even highly automated ones; include some method of displaying the signal to an observer.

- Visual display systems may comprise a calibrated chart and a pointer, an integrated display on a cathode-ray tube, or a digital readout.

- Measurement systems often include elements for recording. A common type utilizes a writing stylus that records measurements on a moving chart. Electrical recorders may include feedback reading devices for greater accuracy.

- The actual performance of measuring instruments is affected by numerous external and internal factors. Among external factors are noise and interference, both of which tend to mask or distort the measurement signal.

- Internal factors include linearity, resolution, precision, and accuracy, all of which are characteristic of a given instrument or system, and dynamic response, drifts, and hysteresis, which are effects produced in the process of measurement itself.

4.19. Expert system in process control

- An expert system is a computer software technique which is best (but not necessarily) implemented using languages and hardware systems from the artificial intelligence stable.

- The software technique offers the potential to encapsulate the experience and knowledge from many human experts and to effectively communicate it to other experts.

- The knowledge is mostly expressed in simple rules from which the expert system makes inferences that lead (to other rules and ultimately) to solutions to problems.

- The feasibility of building real time expert systems for applications in control rooms of process plants has been proven. Companies with sharp forward plans are investing in such systems now in order to obtain early benefits.

- The benefits can manifest themselves in improved security of production which is frequently directly quantifiable as cost savings.

- As expert systems are used as tools to improve the control of operations in other domains (e.g. scheduling, sales and marketing), then ultimately these must be cooperating expert systems.

- An expert system is 'an intelligent automation environment comprised of traditional and heuristic methods to solve a particular problem'. In choosing this definition, I want to emphasis two points. The first is that the 'intelligent automation environment' includes hardware, software and the human experts (i.e. design engineers, process operators, instrument technicians). Certainly the combination of hardware and software is powerful.

- It can process large volumes of data in real time, analyses patterns, recognize trends and suggest control actions.

- These are some attributes of 'intelligence' and they are important in the process control solution. However, the human component is also essential to the 'intelligent control environment'.

- The second point that must be recognized in using expert systems in control strategies is the combination of 'traditional and heuristic methods'.

- Most process control problems will be better solved by a combination of methods rather than a completely heuristic approach. The contribution of the heuristic component will depend upon the particular problem.

- Since expert systems can combine traditional, mathematical methods based on theory as well as operating knowledge in heuristic form that can be applied when the theory doesn't work, it is natural to assume that expert systems have the potential to improve process control.

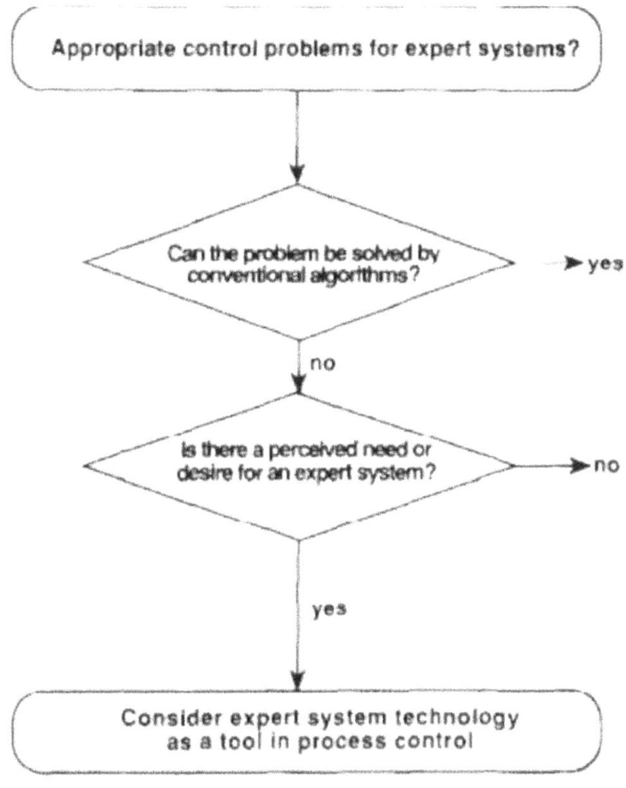

Figure 4.8: Decision algorithm for expert-system technology

4.20. Potential benefits and risks of expert system technology in process control

4.20.1. Benefits

- Can include heuristics/experience factors as well as nonnumeric information in control strategy

- Reduced operator burden

- Can separate knowledge from procedures involved in implementation (i.e. inference engine)

- Tool to allow control system to adapt to changing environmental factors

- Improves overall communications within the plant

4.20.2. Risks

- Risks associated with heuristics and uncertainties in experts' knowledge

- Cannot apply quantitative methodologies

- Cannot be used to develop generalizations of knowledge

4.20.3. Applications

Having analyzed the characteristics of appropriate control problems as well as the risks and benefits of expert systems technology, I will discuss specific areas of application. I think there are three key areas where expert systems can improve process control.

1. Self-tuning controllers: Self-tuning controllers are useful when disturbances change process dynamics, since the controller is able to adapt to these changes. Self-tuning controllers that incorporate expert systems technology are commercially available and have been proven in a number of industrial applications (e.g.

petrochemical and pulp and paper applications). Since the techniques are not industry-specific, the food industry can adopt the technology and there are a number of areas in food processing where self-tuning controllers can be useful.

2. Supervisory expert control: The supervisory control system is developed at a higher level and is capable of integrating the information from individual control loops as well as performing other functions such as analyzing trends in product quality, and assigning causes to quality shifts. You can use expert-system technology at the supervisory level to combine conventional statistical process- control techniques and operator heuristics to make inferences about product quality and relationships between process variables and quality. In addition to overall process supervision, this level of control can include operator support systems.

3. Generation and management of application software for control systems: Sophisticated control hardware and software are commercially available from a number of vendors. However, the implementation of one of these control systems for a specific application still requires a lot of human effort and expertise to formulate control specifications and to produce software for the actual controllers. Development work has started to use expert system and artificial intelligence (AI) techniques to assist in the generation of new application software and software upgrades.

4.21. Fuzzy logic control application in cement plant

- Lotfi Zadeh initiated a Fuzzy Logic technique to resolve uncertain reasoning problems. Therefore, Fuzzy logic is a method to formalize the human capacity of imprecise reasoning, or approximate reasoning. Such reasoning represents the human ability to reason approximately and judge under uncertainty. In fuzzy logic all truths are partial or approximate.

- In this sense, this reasoning has also been termed interpolative reasoning, where the process of interpolating between the binary extremes of true and false represented by the ability of fuzzy logic to encapsulate partial truths.

- Fuzzy Logic applied in industry for process control. Where control applications are the kinds of problems for which fuzzy logic has had the greatest success and acclaim. Many of the consumer products that we use today involve fuzzy control.

- Developers in cement factories need to integrate artificial intelligence techniques such as fuzzy logic. However, technology is not limited on application of Fuzzy Logic.

- Actually, many industrial control systems have features for access over the Internet. As opposed to real-time feedback control, these features are intended for enterprise wide visibility and monitoring purposes.

- Supervisory control and monitoring over the Internet often used rather than real-time feedback control. It is now possible to access process setups and instruments remotely and gain access to real-time data anytime anywhere. The system can be set up for access over the Internet using a web browser.

- Cement industry is one of the process systems trying to be developed. In this case, growing competition forces cement factories to reduce costs, continually increase productivity and quality, reduce the time required for marketing products, and develop technologies and clean production processes based on optimal use of raw materials and energy.

- To achieve these aims, it is necessary to continuously optimize processes, modernize, and develop the systems and facilities.

- In order to avoid human errors and inaccuracies during manual data collection from different parts of the installation, it is wise to avoid wasting human resources through the automation of certain procedures, ensure performance and uniform documentation for all production facilities, provide evaluation reports required and keep records of important data for historical analysis.

4.22. Proposed Approach of Fuzzy logic control

- To evolve the system, we propose a novel approach. Firstly, we applied an artificial intelligence technique, which is fuzzy logic, where we integrated the fuzzy control of different workshops of kiln and the two mills, which ensures that the system is operational at all times, with minimal downtime.

- Secondly, we integrated Internet technology, where the remote control via Internet, used for security of human life and rendering it unnecessary for operators to be at the site for maintenance.

- In addition, when there is a breakdown it is not necessary to send an expert to diagnose and solve the problem because it is difficult to organize visas, flight, etc. Therefore, the proposed system reduces downtimes and travel costs by the possibility of sending reports and transmitting all process data.

- The process control system contains different operators' stations, alarms and trends tables. The operator can execute any operation according to his authentication access. We applied Internet technologies to develop a fuzzy control system based on Internet access for an industrial process plant.

- The system created to optimize the process control in different cement factories in Algeria. Until 2016, none cement industry apply neither fuzzy control nor Internet-based control in his production system. The implementation of the new industrial network architecture programming based on Siemens tools, such as, PCS 7, and Fuzzy Control++.

4.23. Fuzzy logic in cement industry

- The increasing complexity in industrial systems explains the need for monitoring system performance. Security and reliability needs require the implementation of preferment solutions such as artificial intelligence techniques to control industrial processes. One such technique is fuzzy logic.

- For its important value, fuzzy logic developed in several works and applied in different domains.

- In complex systems such as cement manufacturing, one of the proposed fuzzy models is the Takagi-Sugeno (TS) fuzzy model, where fuzzy controllers used for process control can represent non-linear systems.

- FL Smith Automation has been a pioneer in high-level expert control systems for cement kiln applications. It is one of the initiatives applied in cement factories such as SCIMAT in 1987. FLS has a new system based on fuzzy logic used in the cement industry, called ECS/Process Expert (ECS/PXP).

- It is a separate package, initiated after the stabilization of the system. The control system based on the famous industrial platform ECS (Expert Control & Supervision) specially developed for remote monitoring, supervision and reporting.

- ECS/PXP shown in **Figure 4.9** is a solution for control and optimization of complex high-level process, such as baking processes. The control is optimized using advanced functions PxP application, customized to meet the requirements of each user.

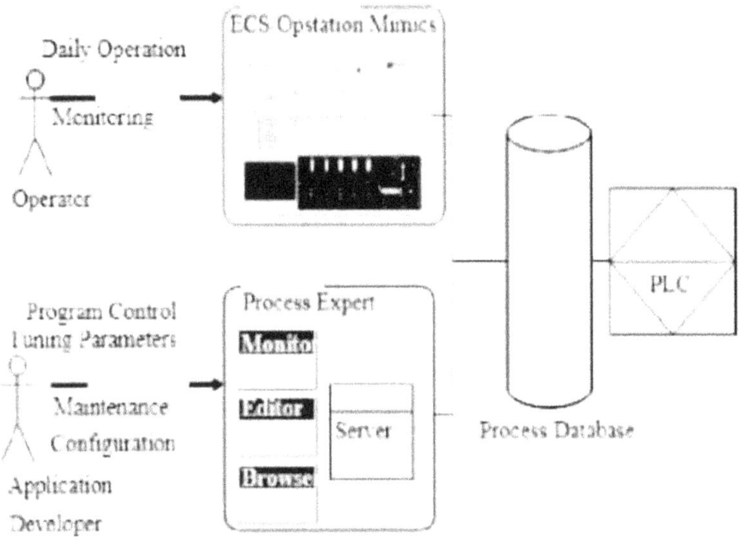

Figure 4.9: ECS/Process Expert

- Depending on the type of application techniques, advanced expert system, fuzzy logic, neural networks, and a predictive model-based controller (MPC), are used in modules Process Expert application to allow patterns of hybrid control to meet the requirements of a given process control.

- These modules carry out regular assessments of complex and process conditions, and perform actions exercising better control and reliability than human operators. The control strategies behind ECS/PXP-

Kiln are based on two decades of experience in cement kiln control and optimization.

4.24. CCR Operator

The CCR operator is responsible for the execution of operation and light maintenance activities under supervision of the shift supervisor.

> **Main Responsibilities and Activities**

- Operates the plant systems from the control room and locally.

- In collaboration with the shift supervisor, arranges his work to ensure there is always someone in the control room.

- Replaces the shift supervisor during his temporary absence from the control room.

- Executes, according to the safety procedures, the necessary precautions and lock - outs.

- Takes readings of plant parameters (tour log), energy and gas, and performs basic chemical water analysis.

- Supervises inventory of plant process chemicals.

- Performs administrative work related to data reporting and operating procedures.

- Helps the chemist in the preparation of all chemical solutions in case of necessity.

- Check the plant regularly, reports malfunctions to the shift supervisor and makes work requests.

- Performs periodic functional tests on plant systems.

- Performs shift turnovers and assures the transfer of the necessary information.

- Makes suggestions for plant and operating procedure improvements.

- Supervises the loading and unloading of chemicals to and from the trucks.

- Responsible for the cleanliness and tidiness of the control room and other rooms used by operations.

- Follows up the availability of operational consumables and reports deviation as needed.

- Reports dangerous hazards on plant systems, work place, working environment and general public.

- Responsible to maintain confidentially of all information available to the position.

- Perform all duties and responsibilities assigned by the immediate supervisor to this position, but not specifically stated in this description.

- Helps to WPTP Operator in case of necessity.

➤ **Supervision**

- There are no related staffs that the main plant operator supervises.

- ➤ **Reporting**
- Reports to the Shift Supervisor.
- ➤ **Environmental Health & Safety Considerations**
- Responsible for performing the operational activities to meet standards of public safety, employee safety and environmental citizenship that meet or exceed regulatory requirements.
- Contacts the fire department in case of fire.
- He is responsible for the implementation of the work permit system and suggests improvements to the H&S officer.
- Reports dangerous hazards on plant systems, work place, working environment and general public.
- Ensures that the plant does not violate any of the environmental rules and report problems.
- ➤ **External Contacts**
- Maintains relations with the power client and the gas supplier.
- ➤ **Skills Required**
- Sufficient technical knowledge in required to manage the plant. Skills Required
- Ability to handle the company's resources (cost) effectively.

- Exercising confidentiality of all information handled.

- Showing initiative and add to a positive working environment.

4.25. Function of CCR in cement plant

- The topic of "Remote Access and Control" in a cement manufacturing facility may initially create apprehension immediately bringing to mind a pyro processing line in operation without any direct control.

- Controlling a pyro-line from a remote site might currently be thought of as unfeasible, but in 10 or 20 years it could be a reality. It was not too long ago when the "burner" who took his post on the burner floor controlled the pyro process system.

- Then came the innovation of the centralized control room. Over the last few years, central control rooms have been located out of sight of the kiln. Currently, control rooms are being sited farther away from the pyro process line.

- Technologies are advancing in areas of computer hardware and software, communications, and industrial networking. These components are becoming the heart of the control systems.

- The idea of remote control is gaining momentum, and like other innovations, it is being advanced in small, manageable steps. This is a subject that is rapidly changing as improvements in communications and computer technologies continue to be made (Vidergar, 1999).

4.26. Working of CCR in Cement plant

- The concept of remote access and control started first with the ability to access software systems from remote locations. In the 1970s there was a desire to have information collected in one location transferred to a different location. This desire is one of the driving forces behind remote control and access.

- The business world embraced remote access as a method of transferring payroll and cost accounting information from the manufacturing site to the central offices. Custom-developed software programs existed on mainframe computers located in the central office. Software users or clients controlled the programs from remote sites and transferred information from the remote site to the central office.

- Communication technology consisted of terminals and modems at the remote site, connected to the mainframe via copper phone wiring, modems, and the telephone companies' communications equipment. Communication speed ranged up to 2400 baud.

- Next, in the 1980s, came the development of maintenance and storeroom inventory systems. These systems enabled the sharing of equipment maintenance information and storeroom inventories between different manufacturing facilities, equipment suppliers, and corporate offices.

- This decade also saw the beginning of the transmission of process data from the manufacturing site. State air quality authorities began to require that process emission data be transmitted to state offices on a routine basis.

- This required software to collect the data from the continuous emission monitoring system (CEMS) and send it to computers in the state offices. In these early systems, the data was collected and stored in a data file. This file was then periodically transmitted to the state agency using early file transfer systems. System security became an issue that had to be managed.

- In the late 1980s, the concept of Computer Integrated Manufacturing (CIM) was also introduced by some in our industry that stressed the need for an expansion of remote access to other areas of manufacturing (DeHayes, 1989).

- These initial systems relied on the user having a terminal in the remote location while all software resided on mainframe computers in a central office.

- Data transfer was a one-way affair. Security was handled at the mainframe. Advancements in communication and computer technologies have enabled faster data transfer rates. Networking technologies began to arrive.

- Internet communication protocols such as Transmission Control Protocol/Internet Protocol (TCP/IP) were developed.

- Modems started to be replaced by hubs, switches, and routers. Equipment now exists which allows local area network (LAN) data transfer rates to 100 mega baud. This is much faster than the 2400 baud rates used 20 years ago. Data transfer rates over the telephone lines increased to 24,400 baud and higher.

- In the 1990s, as telecommunications technologies improved, software also advanced to take advantage of these improved connection speeds.

- Eventually, software was developed to allow personal computers arriving on the scene in the 1980s to be connected to each other and the central office.

- As personal computer technologies improved, they eventually eliminated the previous generation of "dumb" terminals. The PC became useful as a personal productivity tool as well as a terminal to connect to the software packages installed on the central mainframe computers.

- Software progressed by improving existing features and adding new ones. Generally, software is becoming easier to install and use.

- The software developers have improved the human-machine interface through the addition of better mimics and views to the software.

- One of the negative results of these improvements has been software requiring large amounts of computer hard disk memory to store it and large amounts of random access memory (RAM) to operate it.

- The combination of improved communication technologies and software has helped facilitate the improvement in computer hardware.

- The difficulty for consumers is trying to keep up with these technologies improvements, and doing so in a cost-effective manner.

4.27. Process control through CCR in cement plant

- While continued improvements in communications and software occur, improvements to our process control systems are also being developed. Improvements have been realized in processor speeds, graphical interface, and historical data trending.

- The improvements in processor speeds have allowed the system designers to put more features into a control system.

- Control systems evolved from the hardwired relay logic systems as shown in **Figure 4.10** to the computer-based control systems of today, shown in **Figure 4.11**. Once the control systems evolved into the open architecture computer-based systems, the ability to connect to these systems from a remote location became possible.

- Until the mid-1990s, the majority of remote access technology was used in information and business systems.

- The world of process control remained leery, with issues including control system security, stability, and reliability high on the list of reasons not to allow remote access. Eventually, hardware and software were developed to provide a secure access, or firewall, to a process control system.

- The firewall amounted to a protective barrier limiting access to the control system in order to insure that its integrity and responsiveness were maintained.

- Once industry began to accept the idea of remote access to the control system, developers of Programmable Logic Controllers (PLCs) and Distributed Control Systems (DCS) began to include this as a standard feature in their system architecture. Many options now exist regarding remote access.

- Access to the system via dial-up telephone systems or local or wide area networks (LANs and WANs) exists.

Figure 4.10: Control room showing hardwired relay logic systems

Figure 4.11: Control room at a cement manufacturing plant showing computer-based control systems

- Access using corporate intranets or the Internet is available. Techniques used to control access to the system range from controlling when the phone line is connected to using any one of the many software packages available for this purpose. Software packages such as PC Anywhere™, Laplink™, Citrix™, and Microsoft Terminal Server™ all can facilitate access to a remote system, and all have features designed to provide some level of security.

- **Figures 4.12 and 4.13** depict possible methods for remotely connecting to a system. **Figure 4.12** shows three methods to connect to a Foxboro™ DCS control system using the telephone system and the company's WAN.

- The first method attempted (labelled as option 1 in **Figure 4.12**) was using a router and modem supplied by Foxboro™. The router and modem were required on each end of the connection.

- This method was first used in the early 1990s. Connection speeds depended upon the telephone lines, and 9600 to 14,400 baud was considered a good connection. The purpose of the connection was to provide process data at the corporate office for analysis, reporting, and troubleshooting.

- Although, the idea was appealing, the speed of the connection was at times very slow. Also, only one computer in the corporate office could make the connection. Software existed on the control system to recognize the connection and provide data that were requested by the connection.

- A few years later, as PCs and networking technologies improved, a remote access PC was installed on the control system Ethernet highway in the plant (labelled as option 2 in **Figure 4.11**).

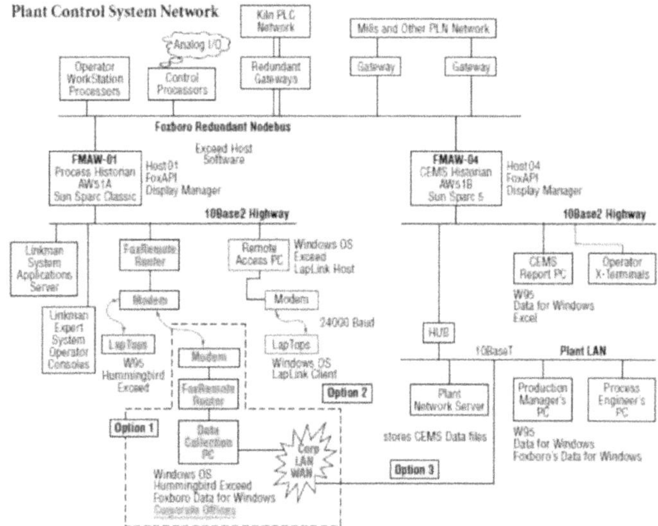

Figure 4.12: Plant control network showing 3 options for connecting to control system

- Software was developed by the control system supplier to allow the PC to have access to the control system network. The PC became a component of the control system while at the same time remaining a stand-alone device.

- With the new multitasking abilities of computers, the PC was able to manage software specific to the control system as well as provide some control system data to the remote access connections. The connection speeds improved to 26 kilo baud.

- Laplink™ software was used to handle login security, and now a computer at any location with Laplink™ software, proper telephone numbers and access codes could connect to the control system.

- The connection speed, while not setting any records, did allow for timely data transfer. In addition to the data being passed to the remote site, it was now possible to monitor system operator mimics in real time. The increased speed of the connection allowed more data to be passed thus allowing operator mimics to be viewed remotely.

- This improved system troubleshooting and process analysis with personnel at the manufacturing site. The limitation to this method of connection was found to be the display manager of the control system only supporting a specific number of connections.

- Because of the control system design limitations, only a specific number of connections (local or remote) could be made at any one time to the system.

- This limited the number of remote access PCs allowed to reside on the system, and this method still only allowed one remote connection at a time through the remote access PC.

- Again, as networking improved, a third route to the system was established (labeled as option 3 on **Figure 4.12**). This route uses the corporate WAN to provide the connection to the plant.

- This method of connecting is similar to that of the second option, But, with this method telephone numbers are no longer required. Internet networking communication protocol (TCP/IP) is incorporated, and each device on the plant and corporate network has its own unique address. By knowing this address, a connection can be made. A portion of the bandwidth on the corporate WAN connection between the corporate office and the plant site is utilized.

- This connection is always open, but only one remote connection at a time is allowed. The network router and the Laplink software provide login security. Connection speeds increased again as these WAN connections can typically transfer data faster than telephone connections.

- **Figure 4.13** shows two remote access connections used with a control system based on PC and server technologies. As with the previous control system example, access to the control system using the Telephone Company and modems provides a basic level of access. Again access is controlled with the connection of the telephone wire along with the software used to dial in.

- In this example, PC Anywhere™ or Laplink™ software packages are used to facilitate the connection and provide login security. These connections are typically used in control system troubleshooting by plant system analysts or the control system supplier.

- The connection can also be used to make changes to the control system PLC logic. This is a useful feature when the plant is located in a remote area, and a situation exists where program changes made over the telephone are much quicker than waiting for the appropriate personnel to travel to the plant.

- The second connection method shown in **Figure 4.13** incorporates another technology improvement over the modem and router connections shown in **Figure 4.12**.

- The second connection in this example uses a remote access server. The purpose of this server is to provide the remote connections with process data, operator mimics, alarming, and trending functions.

- Data can now be exported from the control system into a calculation spread sheet residing on the remote computer. This control system component was designed with remote connections in mind and can support up to 15 remote connections.

- These connections can be remote to the manufacturing site, or they can be onsite plant personnel who want to view the control system from their offices. All connections are made using the plant LAN and corporate WAN.

- It is considered a state-of-the art connection at present. Software in the server coordinates the number of connections, acts as a firewall to the control system, and serves the requested data to the remote users.

- Microsoft terminal server or Citrix™ software products can be used to facilitate the connections.

- In this case, Microsoft Internet Explorer™ is the only software required by the remote user. This eliminates some of the software maintenance required for the system.

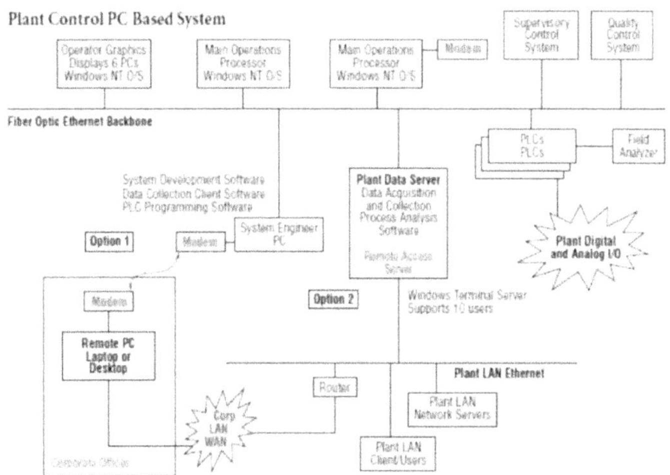

Figure 4.13: Plant control system showing 2 options for connecting to control system

Chapter 5

Process Control advances for Cement Industry

5.1. Roll of electronic device and computer control in cement process

5.1.1. Why measure?

Electrical energy contributes 20-30 % of the cement production cost. Thus electric energy is important factor as a **production component in the cement industry**. It is therefore imperative to measure the energy consumption in order to be able to determine solutions to save energy and thus maintaining the costs at least at the present level.

The energy consumption [kWh] and the specific energy consumption [kWh/t] are even units to compare for example departments in different plants or different types of machines (e.g. ball mill/vertical mill) to each other.

5.1.2. Where to measure?

Drawing E310015 shows the process structure in a cement plant which is ideally represented with the corresponding electrical structure and thus the ideal energy measuring points.

The measuring points are arranged in different levels:

- Main entrance-level; measuring point for charging by Power Company

At this point, the local power company measures the total consumption of the plant; it should also be a comparable-measuring of the plant; but attention, the result has not to be the same (two measuring circuits).

- **Department-level**

Every department should be measured separately to have an overview of the electric consumption in the different departments. Likewise for large consumers which are directly connected to the medium voltage distribution.

- **Process/Non-process-level**

It is necessary to measure the non-process part to distinguish between process- and non-process-consumers. Since less measuring points are used for non-process measurement, costs can be reduced by measuring the Total - non-process = process. (see drawing E310015)

- **Special consumer-level**

This level contains consumers of special interest from an energy point of view.

5.2. Energy/power metering in a cement plant

If all these measuring points are counted together, the total will be around 50. But in practice it is very difficult to find such an electric distribution. So in reality the amount of measuring points will increase to 500 points which will be rather costly. The conclusion is, that measuring starts with **proper electrical departments thus a proper distribution.**

5.2.1. How to measure energy?

Today there are two measurement principles for electric energy, a direct measuring method and an indirect one. - An important criterion is the measuring principle. The method applied depends on the kind of load, the connected voltage (voltage - and/or current transformer necessary) and the accuracy required. The different connection diagrams for the measuring method with kWh-meter. The same principle is utilized for a power transducer.

5.2.2. KWh-meter (direct measuring method)

The kWh-meter forms with the current-path and the voltage-path a mechanical torque, which is proportional to the electric power. This torque sets the metering disc in a corresponding number of turns per unit of time. The multiplication with the time to receive energy follows with the addition of the number of rotations. The kWh-meter shall be equipped with an on/off output module. This module includes a pulse contact system and a pulse amplifier, suitable for further handling in a control system.

For example; in the control system, the energy will be calculated with the time between two pulses. The practice shows that this "digital" method is not such exact than the method described below. The above described measuring method is the principle of "Ferraris"-counter or eddy current motor.

Today more and more static kWh-meters are utilized. The same measuring method is done in an electronic way and not any more in an electro mechanical way, but there is still a pulse contact output.

5.2.3. Power transducer (indirect measuring method)

The power transducer measures current and voltage separately and calculates internally the electric power. The output signal is an analogue signal (4-20 mA) for electric power. *This analogue signal is an input in the control system* where the signal is integrated with the time which results in a more accurate measurement as opposed to a pulse-signal from a kWh-meter.

5.2.4. Process measurement display

The display of the energy measurement is just as important as the measurement itself. The measurement has to be displayed in form of power or energy as well as specific energy measurement (e.g. for the raw mill $\rightarrow$ kWh per ton of raw meal).

5.3. Temperature measurement used in cement plant

In the cement industry generally thermocouples, PT 100 resistance bulbs and pyrometers are used. For kiln shell measurement, temperature scanners are often applied together with a display system. These scanner systems range from a simple pyrometer connected to a recorder or from a scanner head connected to a PC with an elaborated software giving information about the shell temperature, interpretation about the inside of the kiln and even a brick management and slip detection can be included.

5.3.1. Thermocouple

Mostly applied for temperature measurement in the cement industry are thermocouples which use the palter effect as measurement principle. A thermocouple consists of two dissimilar metals. Between these metals a voltage is generated. The electro-motoric force (emf) developed by a thermocouple depends on the temperature of both, the measuring (hot) junction and the reference (cold) junction. Important for a thermocouple is therefore:

- The type of thermocouple and the manufactures data (e.g. type K thermocouple).

- The extension cable of the appropriate type (e.g. type K for type K thermocouple).

- Temperature range and type of thermocouple (e.g. type K for 200 - 1200°C).

- Cold junction reference temperature 0°C, 20°C or others.

- The type of protection sheath. The length of the TC as well as the protection tube should be standardized (e.g. 800 mm and 1200 mm). The material for the sheath may however be different for various applications since a high temperature protection sheath is very expensive.

To calibrate a transmitter for a thermocouple, a mV source is required. This source is connected in the measuring loop instead of the thermocouple. According the manufacturer's data sheet, mV for 0°C and mV for the maximum temperature are fed into the loop. Then the output of the transmitter 0°C = 4 mA and maximum temperature = 20 mA are checked as well as the display in the control room together with any alarm limits. The temperature range from - 200°C up to +2000°C can be covered with thermocouples.

5.3.2. Resistance bulb RTD PT 100

For lower temperature (e.g. for machine protection) resistance thermometers are used. RTD's work on the principle of a resistance changing when the temperature varies, mostly used in the cement industry is the Pt 100 platinum resistance bulb. The PT 100 has a resistance of 100Ω at 0°C and 158.8Ω at 150°C. When selecting a resistance bulb, it is important to specify a 2-, 3- or even a 4-wire type. To compensate for the line resistance a 3 wire type normally is sufficient. If the transmitter is installed nearby, even a 2-wire bulb is good enough.

To calibrate a transmitter for a PT 100 a resistance decade is required. This resistance box is connected in the measuring loop instead of the PT 100. According the data sheet the base resistance (e.g. 100Ω for PT 100) for 0°C and the maximum resistance for the maximum temperature (e.g. 158.8Ω for PT 100) are fed into the loop. Then the output of the transmitter

0°C = 4 mA and maximum temperature = 20 mA are checked as well as the display in the control room together with any alarm limits. PT 100 transmitters require initial calibrations of the entire loop. After that only an occasional check-up is required. With PT 100 bulbs temperatures from -250°C up to +1000°C is measurable.

5.3.3. Pyrometer

The cement industry uses two types of pyrometers. The radiation pyrometer which detects radiation through an optical lens system onto the thermopile or photo cell and the two colour ratio pyrometer which compares the ratio of the radiation intensity of two different wave lengths.

5.3.4. Scanner

The central feature of a scanner is a motor driven optical system which scans the entire kiln with a certain frequency (e.g. 16 Hz). The front of the scanner measures parallel along the axis of the kiln, in the back of the scanner a reference temperature is used to calibrate the system.

5.4. Pressure Measurement Instruments

Pressure can be measured either as liquid column (e.g. U-tube) with a mechanical principle (e.g. diaphragm, burden tube) or electrically (e.g. piezo crystal, strain gauge). The pressure measured in the cement industry is usually very low. Therefore, the differential pressure (gage pressure that is the difference between the absolute pressure and the atmosphere) is measured. Most pressure transmitters applied in the cement industry are of the mechanical type where one side is connected to the process and the other side is left open to the atmosphere.

Drawing F44570-1 is a typical example of a differential pressure measurement. The bellows are subjected to a pressure change and move, via mechanical links, a plunger in an electrical field. The electronic senses the movement and converts the change in the field into an electrical standard signal.

To avoid problems with pressure transmitters some installation points have to be observed:

Location: locate the transmitter near the pressure tapping easy accessible, Mostly applied as unit by the manufacturer.

Process line: The pressure tapping can be above or below the transmitter. In any case the process line must be installed such that no water or dirt can accumulate. Thus, always have at least 2% slopes in the process line. If the tapping is above the transmitter a water trap is required.

Tapping: Install a tapping in such a way that cleaning is easily possible. Thus, a simple removable cover should allow pocking of the process tapping. In large ducts two or more tapings connected with each other give a better result.

To calibrate a pressure transmitter a pressure source is required. This source is connected in the measuring loop on the primary side of the transmitter. To check the zero both sides of the transmitter are left open to the atmosphere. To check the maximum, an equivalent pressure (or vacuum) is applied. The output of the transmitter 0 kPa = 4 mA and maximum pressure = 20 mA are checked as well as the display in the control room together with any alarm limits.

5.5. Flow (liquid, gas) Measurement Instruments

Flow measurements are normally indirect measurements using differential pressures to measure the flow rate. Flow measurements can be divided into the following groups: flow rate, total flow, and mass flow. The choice of the measuring device will depend on the required accuracy and fluid characteristics (gas, liquid, suspended particulates, temperature, viscosity, and so on.)

Flow rate: Differential pressure measurements can be made for flow rate determination when a fluid flows through a restriction. The restriction produces an increase in pressure which can be directly related to flow rate. The commonly used restrictions; (a) Orifice plate, (b) Venturi tube, (c) Flow nozzle, and (d) Dall tube.

Total flow: Includes devices used to measure the total quantity of fluid flowing or the volume of liquid in a flow. Positive displacement meters use containers of known size, which are filled and emptied for a known number of times in a given time period to give the total flow volume. Two of the more common instruments for measuring total flow are the piston flow meter and the notating disc flow meter.

Mass flow: By measuring the flow and knowing the density of a fluid, the mass of the flow can be measured. Mass flow instruments include constant speed impeller turbine wheel-spring combinations that relate the spring force to mass flow and devices that relate heat transfer to mass flow.

Anemometer is an instrument that can be used to measure gas flow rates. One method is to keep the temperature of a heating element in a gas flow constant and measure the power required. The higher the flow rate, the higher the amount of heat required.

The alternative method (hot-wire anemometer) is to measure the incident gas temperature and the temperature of the gas downstream from a heating element; the difference in the two temperatures can be related to the flow rate. Micro-machined anemometers are now widely used in automobiles for the measurement of air intake mass.

The advantages of this type of sensor are that they are very small, have no moving parts, pose little obstruction to flow, have a low thermal time constant, and are very cost effective along with good longevity.

5.6. Liquid Level Measurement

Level measurements, whether continuous or just as level alarms are often applied and often not 100% satisfactory. A poll carried out in 1992 querying the performance of the different level measurements in some 30 factories showed results from very satisfactory to useless.

Depending on the method applied, the installation and the maintenance the same level measurement is rated different with regards to performance. The following level measurements are used successfully in the cement industry. Some mechanical types like paddle, ball etc. are not explained since their function are very simple.

5.7. Capacity probe measurements

The capacity probe uses the measuring principle of two plates being isolated by a dielectric ε where the capacitance depends on the area of the plates, the distance between the plates and the medium between the plates the dielectric. When installing a capacity probe, the plates (the probe and the silo wall) are fixed and the distance is fixing provided, the probe is mounted properly.

The variation in the measuring loop is therefore the dielectric ε which is formed either by material between probe and wall or air. The following problems may occur thus hampering the performance:

- Sticky material on the probe. This can be avoided using the proper type of level probe that is insulated or partly insulated probes.
- Probe installed too close to silo wall thus evoking bridging.
- Sensitivity adjusted to fine. Humidity in the air or in the material changes the property of the dielectric.
- Mechanical damage may result from coarse material or from sheer force. (E.g. coal dust has very high sheer force). Use another measuring principle or use an insulated capacity probe.

5.8. Vibration measurements

The vibration fork level probe is only used for a single point measurement. A driver induces a vibration in the probe and a controller senses a change when material dampens the vibration. The tuning fork is obtainable in two forms, one being the actual fork and the other in form of a tube. The following problems may occur thus hampering the performance:

- Material stuck between the forks. Use a tube type to avoid this problem mostly occurring with coarse material.

- Material coating the probe. Use the fork type probe since this problem takes place mainly with fine material.

5.9. Electro mechanical measurements

Quite successful practice is the level measurement with the so called silo pilot. A rope or measuring tape connected to a weight is lowered into the silo. As soon as the weight touches the material surface, the rope (tape) tension ceases, the motor reverses and pulls the weight back into its original position. During the upward travel the tape is measured, such giving an indication of the level within the silo. The following points have to be considered by using a silo pilot:

- Position on top of the silo so that no material can fall onto the weight. When lowering the weight it should be in the center of the material cone.

- Access to the rope respective belt and the weight must be easy. Install an inspection door to assist maintenance.

- Select the proper weight for the corresponding material.

5.10. Contactless level probes measurements

Several methods allow level measurement without being in contact with the material. Ultra sonic is the most popular and is used with coarse material, e.g. gypsum, limestone. In connection with dust in the sonic beam or on the material surface <40°C, e.g. cement, raw meal, this method should not be applied.

Level can be measured up to 45 m under good conditions. Rather new on the market are infrared and radar. With infrared no experience has been gained. Good experiences have been gained with radar in environment where ultrasonic fails.

In clinker and in raw material silos the measurement with radar proved to be successful even with high dust load. In raw meal the measurement did not work and the problem seems to be the conductivity.

Only material with certain conductivity respective a low dielectric can reflect the radar beam. Up to now only measurements for 35 m depth are available. This is due to the strength of the source which must be within the limit of the wireless regulation of the respective country. The radar method works in a temperature range of -40°C up to +250°C.

5.11. Radiation level probes measurements

Well-known and well-proven are the nuclear type of level probes. From a measurement technical point of view no restrictions are known. In most cases where all other methods fail the nuclear level probe serves well almost maintenance free.

In many countries, however, importing or handling the source is very difficult. Additionally the disposal of the source is in many cases almost impossible and requires a lot of responsibility of the person in charge. And more restriction for the future is to be expected.

An alternative (even in the pre-heater cyclones) offers the micro wave level measurement. The arrangement is similar to the nuclear level measurement a microwave source on the one side and a detector on the other side. The microwaves beam of approx. 20° angle, some 5.8 GHz or as high as 24.125 GHz penetrate any non-conductive material.

The maximum distance through air is around 8 m. Alternative measurements around the corner are possible if the space is limited. The installation must be such that a light beam would be properly reflected.

Microwave level measurements are sensitive to moisture. In fact, microwave is used as well for moisture measurement. The microwave source is so weak, that no danger comes from the measurement. (No cooking can be done with this microwave source; the energy emitted is less than 25 mW.)

5.12. Weight measurement in cement plant

Weighing and weigh feeder play an important role in the cement industry. To produce a good cement quality, accurate weigh feeding of the different components is important. To bill the customer agreeable again, weighing plays the key role.

Already these two important requirements show that for weighing two different ways are possible: the static weighing (weigh bridge) and the dynamic weighing (weigh feeder).

The weigh bridge at the factory entrance is regarded as the most important and accurate unit. The weigh bridge is in many countries subjected to stringent government regulation and must be checked and calibrated on a regular base. For weigh bridges the measuring principle applied is usually one or several load cells. Due to the strict government roles and due to the simple measurement principle these scales usually are fairly accurate.

Small bins are as well placed onto load cells to weigh the contents. And, as long as the construction is suitable, that is three load cells, free moving construction and protection against wind, the measurement can be very accurate.

The total weight (xy tons in the bin) may not be accurate but loss in weight is accurate. Thus, for calibration of a weigh feeder or for volumetric weigh feeding a loss in weight is well-qualified.

The next important weighing principle is the continuous measurement of material to constantly feed an accurate amount of material, the dynamic weighing with weigh feeder. Several principles are applied with different accuracy, different efforts for maintenance and different prices.

Thus when selecting the weigh feeder the following points must be taken into consideration:

- Accuracy required.

- Mechanical suitability for the material and the environment.

- Space availability (height and area). Especially building height can be reduced (cost saving) with certain weighing arrangements and weighing principles.

- Signal availability and signal transmission. (4-20 mA and digital signals or communication via a bus system).

- Maintenance that is time interval between calibrations, access for calibration e.g. rerouting of material onto a lorry, cleaning required, complexity of the control, spare parts etc.

- Measurement principle.

- Silo discharge system. Most problems of inaccurate weighing arise from poor flowing material.

5.13. Belt weigher in cement plant

The most common measuring principle applied in the cement industry is the belt weigher. A section of the belt runs over idlers supported by a frame section placed onto load cells. The weight over this belt section multiplied with the speed represents the feed rate

$$Q = P * v \qquad (5.1)$$

Whereas:

Q = feed rate [t/h]

P = weight per width [kg/m]

v = speed [m/h]

This principle is well-known and if maintained properly very accurate (error < 1%)

Also different methods of calibration are offered, but only the following are accurate and repeatable: Run for e.g. 5 minutes material onto a lorry, weigh the lorry and calculate the feed rate weight x 12 (if the calibration time was 5 min.).

Thus when designing the weigh feeders a means to calibrate onto a lorry must be included or alternatively weigh bins above the feeders to calibrate with the loss in weight method which is a very accurate method too.

5.14. Gravimetric feed system in cement plant

A gravimetric feed system is mainly used for coal feeders. This weighing system is complex but accurate. A bin on load cells is rapidly charge with material. The filling then stops and for n seconds the bin is emptied. When reaching a certain low level the bin is recharged again and during this time the speed of the discharge feeder is maintained at the previous feed rate.

Modern systems calculate the feed rate during a very short time period and take the whole time to calibrate the system. The accuracy of such a system is < 1%. The maintenance however is high and the system is complex.

5.15. Volumetric feeders in cement plant

A simple method is a volumetric feeder. The accuracy is largely dependent on the feeder itself and on the flow property of the material. Depending on the required accuracy, a periodic calibration onto a lorry is needed. If a higher accuracy is required a weigh bin has to be introduced prior to the feeder and a similar measuring method as mentioned in the gravimetric flow measurement has to be applied.

5.16. Impact flow meter in cement plant

A controversial measurement is the weight measurement with an impact flow meter. Material flows on to a plate which in turn is placed on a load cell. The impact on to the plate is proportional to the impact created by a mass falling from a height h. The impact is in practice also depending on the flow properties of the material which in turn is depending on various factors. Thus, this measurement requires a fair amount of mechanical design around the actual measurement. Deducting, the feed to and away from the impact flow meter are crucial for the accuracy of the measurement.

In practice the impact flow meter is mostly applied together with a pre bin arranged with load cells. This arrangement allows an automatically periodical calibration of the flow meter, in order to compensate sticking material at the plate.

5.17. Nuclear weigh feeder in cement plant

Weighing with nuclear weigher is nothing new in the cement industry but is and remains a controversial measurement. Although, a simple and reliable measurement the import and the disposal of the nuclear source is problem. A nuclear weigher consists of a gamma source and a gamma ray detector. Both are connected on a mechanical frame which is located across the conveyor. The beauty is that almost any conveyor (e.g. belt, apron feeder, screw conveyor etc.) can be fitted with an A or C frame nuclear weigher. Even in an existing installation does the installation of an A or C frame seldom present a problem.

A nuclear weigh feeder determines the weight by measuring the absorption of the material. Every material absorbs radiation according the exponential law. The absorption is proportional to the thickness and the density of the material bed. The absorption is then related to the mass of the material which, when multiplied with the speed, results in the mass flow.

The main absorption (basic absorption Ag) is in many cases given by the construction. The absorption with a given density is then proportional with the bed thickness (Am). To receive good results the absorption Ag should not be larger than 95%. Due to a less thick material bed and the absorption measured by the detector is lower. The absorption by the conveyor is remaining constant and calibrated as zero.

When installing a nuclear weigher the following points should be taken into consideration:

- Import regulation for nuclear devices.
- Disposal of nuclear sources
- Building and conveyor construction
- Basic absorption (Ag)
- Electronic with source decay compensation
- Even material flow (an irregular bed which influences the measurement negatively).
- The initial accuracy is around 2% remaining constant even with hardly any maintenance.

5.18. Head flow meter in cement plant

In an air lift the air pressure measured is more or less proportional to the amount of material transported. However, pressure influence other than the amount of material is coming from deducting and from pressure changes from the system following the air lift (e.g. pre-heater and kiln). The head flow meter as an indication to the material flow is quite acceptable.

5.19. Power measurement in cement plant

In the cement industry, the topic "Energy" will become more and more important. In the past until today the price for electrical energy is still low enough that nobody cares too much. But the near future will show us the opposite.

The energy consumption will still increase but the energy production cannot follow this rising demand. Thus a bottle-neck will occur. The power companies have already started to think about increasing energy prices and how to introduce new tariff structures (Energy Exchange). Consequently, we have at least to stabilize our energy consumption or, even better, decrease the consumption. The first step will be to **measure** before other steps can be taken.

5.19.1. What is electrical energy?

Energy, generally, is stored work or the ability to perform work. Electric energy (W_{el}) is potential energy or expressed in another way, the product of electric voltage (U) and electric charge (Q). The electric charge can be replaced by the product of current and time:

$$W_{el} = U * Q = U * I * t \qquad (5.2)$$

Where, I = current and t = time

The electric energy is comparable to energy of position in the mechanic that is:

- Potential difference: height -> voltage U.

- Quantity: weight -> electric charge Q.

The unit is volt-ampere-second [VAs] or in a more practical way kilo-watt-hour [kWh]. One kWh is equal to 3.6 MJ [860 kcal].

5.19.2. What is electric power?

To express performance the work to complete is related to the time required to do it. Similar, the more powerful a machine is, the more work can be done in a shorter time. Thus, the power is proportional to the work and inverse proportional to the time to complete the job. The electric power (P) is the product of voltage (U) and current (I). At the first sight, there is no time any more in the formula, but the definition of the current is the relation between the transported charge quantity and the time. The electric power is comparable to the mechanical power. For example, the power of a hydro power plant is dependent on the height of fall (voltage) and the flux (current).

- The unit is volt-ampere [VA] or more practical kilo-watt [kW].

5.19.3. Apparent, actual and reactance

The power companies bill in most cases the actual energy only. To avoid producing too much apparent energy, they demand a power factor correction between 0.87 and up to 0.9. Few power companies ask for a reactance energy meter and if certain values are surpassed adjust the bill accordingly. Some power companies bill the client already according the apparent energy (measured actual and reactive energy). And this may be the future method of accounting the client since a power company has to produce the apparent power and not only the actual power.

Using a mechanical diagram the three electrical components: apparent (resultant), actual (linear) and reactive (lateral) are explained. The following picture explains the three different electrical components, apparent, actual and reactive current. Whether current, power or energy is used is immaterial for this example.

When looking at the force diagram the energy required pulling the spring is obviously the linear force F_p (electrical actual force). The spring is subjected to the following two forces:

- The lateral force FQ (electrically reactive force) which is not required.
- The resultant force F (electrically apparent force) has to be produced in order to gain sufficient momentum to pull the spring apart.

When measuring an electric circuit with a transducer the actual power is measured which is required to drive a machine. The power company in turn produces the apparent power. If the cosine ϕ is multiplied with the apparent power, the result is the actual power. The difference between the produced and the consumed power is the reactive power.

Apparent power $S = U * I$ (5.3)

[VA] or [kVA]

Actual power $P = U * I * \cos \phi$ (5.4)

$P = S * \cos \phi$ (5.5)

[W] or [kW]

Reactive power $Q = U * I * \sin \phi$ (5.6)

[var] or [kvar]

5.20. Programmable Logic Controller (PLC) in cement plant

- A Programmable Logic Controller (PLC) is nowadays key component for Industrial Automation. PLC helps in making the automation more flexible.

- The PLC is a programmable device, which executes functions such as logic, timing, counting, arithmetic operations and data manipulations.

- It continuously monitors the status of input devices, processes the input data as programmed, makes decisions and modifies the outputs accordingly. The program stored in the memory can be readily modified.

- The novelty of PLC is that it can operate in an industrial environment with temperature ranging from 0 to $60^{O}C$ and humidity ranging from 0 to 90%.

- The use of PLCs with power electronics in electric machine applications has been introduced in the manufacturing automation.

- Many factories use PLCs in automation processes to diminish production cost and to increase quality and reliability. PLC continuously monitors the inputs and activates the outputs according to the control program.

- The PLC correlates the operational parameters to the requested by the user and monitors the system during normal operation and under trip conditions.

5.21. PLC as a system controller

For clinker formation squirrel cage induction motor is commonly used. Required speed range is of the order of 1:10. Starting torque required is about 200-250% of rated torque. Process temperatures can reach as high as $1450^{\circ}C$ during the clinker making process.

For the purpose analog output of PLC is varied from 0-10 V by using move block in the PLC ladder logic. For a 12 bit processor 4096 corresponds to 10 V is set. To provide stepped variation of speed, a timer is used and analog output voltage is varied in steps.

Continuous voltage variation can also be done to achieve continuous speed variation. Motor speed is sensed using proximity sensor which is connected to one input of the PLC. A counter, timer, multiplier and move blocks of PLC is required to calculate the motor speed. The no. of pulses for a fixed time interval is counted by the PLC and converted into speed in RPM.

Speed of the motor is sensed continuously and simultaneously. Once the speed goes beyond limit a trip signal is given to stop the motor. Temperature of the motor is sensed using scale with parameter (SCP) block and RTD output. If the sensed temperature is beyond limit, a trip signal is given to stop the motor.

Also various protections like single phasing, material availability, door guard, conveyor on, lubricating oil pump on, cooling fan on etc. are provided. In case any condition is not fulfilled the motor cannot operate. Motor current is measured using current transducer and analog input of the PLC.

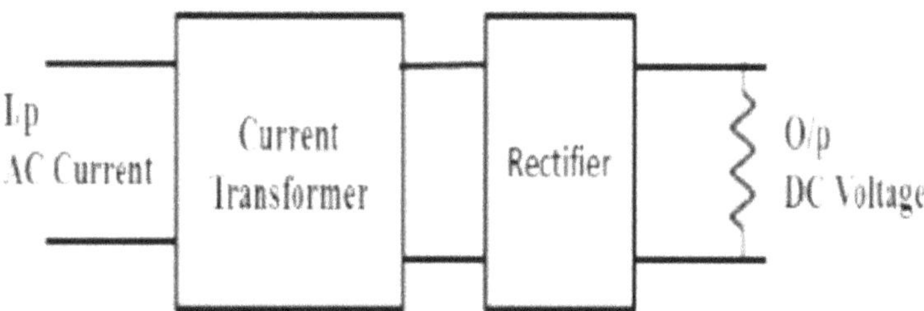

Figure5.1: Block diagram of Current Transducer

In **Figure5.1** AC current is first stepped down using current transformer and then using rectifier ac current is converted to DC current. By using one resistance this DC current is converted to DC voltage which can be fed to analog input of PLC. This DC voltage is calibrated to corresponding AC motor current. Once the motor is overloaded a trip signal is given to motor through PLC.

5.22. Direct digital control (DDC) in cement plant

- A control study of the cement manufacturing process has culminated in the installation of a direct digital control (DDC) system which automatically controls both the ball-mill blending of raw materials for kiln feed and the kiln-cooler combination.

- In each case, the control schemes were developed by determination of the process dynamics, computer simulation and analysis, and field application at the plant.

- The blending control scheme finally developed is based on measurement of ball-mill output composition with an X-ray analyser, and on a concept of non-interacting feed forward-feedback control.

- The kiln-cooler control scheme utilizes conventional and advanced control techniques such as nonlinear, feed forward and adaptive compensations, and optimization.

- This control scheme includes coordinated loops for control of burning zone temperature by manipulation of fuel rate and/or kiln speed, for control of kiln exit temperature and oxygen by ID fan speed, and for maximization of production rate by trim manipulation of kiln speed.

- The control schemes are being applied at the plant with a DDC system which provides maximum operating flexibility with extensive simplification of the operator-computer interface. The direct digital control operating experience has been very favorable.

5.23. Distributed Control Systems (DCS) in cement plant

- Recent developments within the cement industry have seen widespread implementation of computational technologies into the automation of production processes.

- Many recently built or renovated medium and large-scale cement product lines have adopted Distributed Control Systems (DCS). Unfortunately, many of the smaller plants aren't up to speed technologically, rather depending heavily on traditional instrumentation. Some such plants monitor and control the process manually.

- The inauspicious setup at these sites hinders product quality and quantity; it also keeps plants from saving energy, reducing consumption and being competitive.

- The cost of large-scale DCS systems is so high that these firms can't afford it. In order to solve these problems we have developed a new DCS system that is lower in cost and have implemented it in our plant.

5.24. System Software of Distributed Control Systems

- Because of the complexity of the system requirements, which include friendly HMI and real-time monitoring and control, we develop the control software for IPC in Visual Basic 5.0 for Windows.

- The software is composed of a system management module, a simulation display module of process flow diagraming, a simulation display module of the instrument screen, database management module, data communication module, control algorithm module etc. The use of many ActiveX controls in the software greatly reduces development time.

- We used the library files provided by ICPDAS for the I-7188 in QuickBasic during the development of the software. About 200KB of memory is enough for performing control functions.

- And the software is composed of data processing and data communication modules. The system of the formation of a ball of raw material includes a function module, which can implement the conversation between human and machine.

5.25. SCADA and its application in cement plant

- Automation of manufacturing operations helps in increasing the production, improving the product quality, enhancing the safety of the operators as their role get transformed to supervisors and decreasing the cost of production.

Types of Automation and Relevant Control Systems

It is common practice to divide automation into three "levels" as below:

Level 1: Digital controllers and complete process controllers with control and logic functionality (PLC systems).

Level 2: Plant control of sub processes for yield optimization, using advanced sensors (automatic analysers, etc.) directly in the process (raw material characterization, stockpile monitoring, and grade control, raw mix control, and optimization, etc.).

These would include XRF, XRD, and PGNAA systems positioned on conveyor belts, at process inputs or outputs such as after secondary crushers, before and after mills, and so on.

Level 3: This includes automated systems for production coordination/collaboration within the entire process department or the entire manufacturing operation of the plant. The objective is to minimize total costs while maximizing yields and quality control.

A fully functional vehicle would include computational capacity for superordinate production control and sub process simulation facilities. Requirements also involve, at minimum, the capacity for both controlling and monitoring control functions simultaneously.

- SCADA systems became popular to arise the efficient monitoring and control of distributed remote equipment.
- SCADA systems became popular to arise the efficient monitoring and control of distributed remote equipment.
- Today SCADA systems include operator level software applications for viewing, supervising and

troubleshooting local machines and process activities. Powerful software technologies are used for controlling and monitoring equipment.

5.26. SCADA implementation in cement plant

SCADA graphics screens are developed for cement clinker formation process. In **Figure 5.2** main screen contains status of wound rotor induction motor (ON/OFF) used for clinker formation, status of supply (ON/OFF), duration of motor running, system status (healthy/unhealthy), actual motor speed, motor winding temperature, running duration of motor etc.

One rectangle is animated for ON/OFF switch of Cement Kiln motor. Motor running status is animated using motor picture; it turns green in running condition of motor otherwise red. System healthy condition and supply ON/OFF condition are animated using circles.

Using Numerical display actual running duration of the Cement Kiln motor is displayed. Using numerical input enable, in run time maximum temperature of the motor can be changed and also the actual temperature of the motor is displayed using numerical display.

Alarm for analog signals like temperature, motor current and motor speed is set. If the temperature of motor winding exceeds beyond limit one banner displaying temperature high will appear on the main graphics window. Once the alarm is acknowledged, acknowledged (ack) alarm button should be clicked. And if the alarm is attended it can be cleared by clicking at clear alarm button. Similarly alarm trigger values for motor speed and motor current are set.

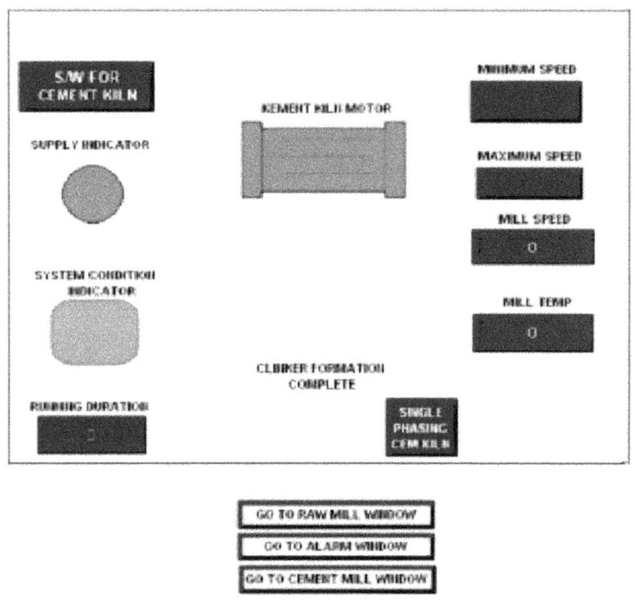

Figure5.2: SCADA graphics window for Cement Kiln

Faulty conditions are displayed in the form of alarm banners. On these banners time of alarm, acknowledged or not, time of acknowledgement are mentioned. Speed limits of the motor are tagged on the SCADA screen using numerical input enable. Before switching ON the motor, speed limit can be changed in run time. And the actual speed of the Cement Kiln motor is displayed using numerical display.

On the main graphics window of Cement Kiln, navigation buttons are provided for different windows. These are GO TO alarm window, GO TO Raw mill window, GO TO cement mill window. Using these buttons we can monitor other process in run time on the graphics window. Alarms can be cleared separately by clicking at clear alarm or all together at once by clicking at clear all alarms.

Reference Books

1. Cement Data Book: W. H Duda , Verlag G m Bh,Berlin

2. Cement Industry Data Book, CAM , New Delhi

3. Chemical process control: Stephnopolous, G . PHI 1990

4. Process System analysis and Control: Coughnower, McGraw Hill, 1991

5. Principle of measurement systems: Bently J P, Longmans.

6. Principle of Industrial Instrumentation: Patranabis, D, TMH